Betta Fish

or

Siamese Fighting Fish

Betta Fish Owner's Manual

Betta fish care, health, tank, costs and feeding.

by

Edward Eldington

Published by: IMB Publishing

Table of Contents

Chapter 1: Introduction

The Betta (*Betta splendens*) fish is better known in some countries as the Siamese fighting fish. In Thailand, one of its countries of origin, it is called the *pla-kad*, which translates as "biting fish". The Betta is a species of gourami known for both its beauty and levels of aggression.

As with some other fish species, the Betta looks very different in its natural habitat where it has short fins and drab colours. It is only when they become agitated that the strong, vibrant colours emerge in wild specimens.

It is this ability to change colour that breeders have manipulated and the domesticated Betta boasts glorious hues all the time. There is now a wide range of colours and fin and tail shapes to delight the aquarist. These fish are also bred very successfully in captivity, including by hobbyists.

This book will introduce you to these vibrant fish by looking at the different types, discussing their appearance and biology, typical Betta fish behaviour, their feeding requirements, and what makes these elegant fish both fascinating and unique.

It will also tell you what you need to know in order to decide whether or not this is the pet for you and, if it is, where to buy one, how to select your Betta fish, what you need to buy before you bring it home, and how to take proper care of it.

The hobbyist also has to know what these fish need with regards to their environment. All the necessary equipment and water and other parameters are examined, as the quality of the water and the general environment have a crucial bearing on the health and happiness of Betta fish.

Like all fish, the Betta is unfortunately susceptible to a number of different types of bacterial, parasitic and fungal infections and infestations. Anyone who is serious about having a fish tank needs to know what to look for and how to deal with common fish ailments.

This book contains helpful information on their mating behaviour, spawning and on caring for the hatchlings or fry for those who are interested in breeding one or more of the Betta fish species.

Please note that some of the information in this book is not specific to the Betta fish. I hope that you find this book both useful and enjoyable to read!

Chapter 2: Betta fish basics

1) Betta fish overview

The Betta fish is native to Asia. More specifically, the species is endemic to Cambodia, Vietnam, Laos and Thailand (formerly known as Siam). These small fish are found in the shallow waters of floodplains, ditches, slow-moving streams and even rice paddies.

It is believed that the Betta, a fish prone to aggression towards other fish, got its name from a clan of fierce Asian warriors called the "Bettah". In addition to being given this name, these fish were also known as *pla-kad* and "The Jewel of the Orient". Currently, the most commonly used name is the Siamese Fighting Fish.

Records indicate that these small fish were caught and collected by people in the 1700 and 1800's. In the wild, Bettas are dull-looking fish: grey, green or even brown in colour and with fairly short fins. Fish captured during this period were certainly not desirable because of their appearance or as pets. It was their feisty natures that made them popular initially.

Wild Bettas only fight for very brief periods before one of them will retreat. However, in the 1800's they were bred for fighting. However, the notion that these were "fights to the death" is an exaggeration as it is rare that this would occur. The weaker fish would back away before either combatant was too seriously injured. The aim of the contest was to decide which fish was braver, not to kill or maim either.

The king of Thailand himself was a great enthusiast who collected and licenced Bettas. He also regulated and taxed the sport. In the mid 1800's he presented one of his prized fighting fish to an eminent Danish physician, botanist and zoologist, Dr Theodore Cantor, who had spent a great deal of time doing research in Asia. A decade later Dr Cantor wrote an article about these fish and he gave them the name *Macropodus pugnax*.

The 1890's saw Betta fish being imported into both Germany and France. Importers in Paris and Berlin respectively then sold them to a growing number of collectors and hobbyists. In 1909 Charles Tate Regan, a British ichthyologist, renamed the domesticated betta fish *Betta splendens.*

These splendid fish are now very popular but unfortunately can be mistreated and even allowed to die thanks to some myths about them. These will be discussed a little later.

2) Life span or expectancy

Bettas in tanks or aquariums generally live for 2 to 3 years but can reach the age of 7. There have been a few reports of Betta fish living in captivity into their teens but these are certainly the exception and not the rule.

Life expectancy, as with most other species of fish, is largely determined by two things: exposure to diseases and parasites before the fish is sold and the care the new owner takes of the fish thereafter.

A poor health history can be overcome to a degree by a responsible and careful hobbyist. Diet, environment and medical care are all key factors in ensuring a long and healthy life for any fish, including the Betta.

3) Betta fish anatomy

Basics:

The Betta is a small fish with a standard length of approximately 6.5 centimetres or 2.6 inches.

Like all fish, the Betta fish has a head, body, tail and fins. As with the majority of fish species, the two eyes are set on either side of the head and so are the nostrils or, to use the correct term, nares.

What is unusual about the Betta is the way it has adapted to environmental conditions. As previously mentioned, the Betta fish lives in shallow waters in Asia, a region known for both torrential rains and flooding and terrible droughts. These remarkable fish have evolved to become labyrinth fish.

This means that they have the ability to both take in oxygen directly from the air and through its gills. The result of this ability is that Betta fish can survive for *short* periods out of water. The primary mechanism for breathing, however, remains the gills.

Gills:

Another feature shared with other fish is the gills, through which they breathe. The gills are located on either side of the body, just behind the head and are curved. Most fish have 8-gill slits (4 per side) and the gills inside them function like lungs. The covering over the gills is called the operculum.

The gills are complex structures and they absorb oxygen molecules from the water that passes over them. Again similar to lungs, carbon dioxide is released from the gills. When a fish opens and closes its mouth it is actually pumping water in so that it can flow over the gills, allowing this vital exchange of gases.

In addition to the absorption of the oxygen, which is essential to life, the gills also regulate the amount of salt or sodium absorbed. Within the gills themselves there are highly specialised cells called, appropriately, chloride cells. These cells are able to excrete the excess salt in the fish's body. Fresh water fish like the Betta, not surprisingly, have far fewer of these cells in their gills than marine fish that live in saline or salt waters.

Fins:

Bettas also have the standard types of fins, although some of the larger and more flowing fins can hinder movement rather than helping with it. Each fin serves a different purpose, enabling movement in specific directions:

- The dorsal fins are located on the back of the fish and their purpose is to help fish maintain balance and stability when they swim. The rear dorsal fin is soft whereas the larger, front dorsal fin is spiny and more rigid.

- The ventral or pelvic fins are found in the pelvic region of the fish. Like the dorsal fins, the pectorals promote stability and balance.
- The pectoral fins are located on either side of the fish, just behind the operculum. They allow side-to-side movements and allow the fish to manoeuvre through the water.
- The caudal fin is also called the tail. This fin is larger than the others and its purpose is to propel the fish through the water.

Bettas bred in captivity sport a dazzling array of tail and fin types, which will be examined in detail later.

Gender:

With many species the male is far more colourful than the female and this is often a reliable way to tell the one gender from the other. This is not the case with Betta fish, as the genetic changes and mutations that have resulted from careful in-captivity breeding mean that – usually – both males and females have vibrant, glowing colours.

However, it is still easy to tell a female from a male Betta fish. Firstly, females are smaller than their male counterparts. Secondly, it is only males that have long, flowing fins; those of female fish are shorter. The final gender marker is a behavioural one, as males are much more aggressive and territorial than females.

4) Betta varieties

Some breeders have tried to use Betta fish to create hybrids by crossing *Betta splendens* with other varieties of Betta. The other members of the Betta genus that have been used, with varying degrees of success, are *Betta smaragdina*, *Betta imbellis*, *Betta raja* and *Betta mahachaiensis*. Other breeders have stepped outside the Betta genus and used the *Macropodus operculis* or Paradise Fish.

A type of Betta that made its appearance on the hobby and aquarist markets fairly recently is the King Betta. The origin and therefore genetics of this variety is unknown, which means they present problems in terms of breeding with them.

The essential and superficial differences between the King and *Betta splendens* are size (the King is far larger) and colour, because Kings have a very limited colour range (rich beige to white).

5) Types of Betta fins and tails

In addition to the variety, thanks to careful breeding and the creation of genetic hybrids, *Betta splendens* is found in an extraordinary range of both colours and fin shapes.

Aquarists and even those who don't keep fish are more familiar with the very popular veil tail. However, most fish shops and online retailers stock the following types of Bettas:

- Veil tail: the fins are very long and flowing and the tail is not symmetrical; unlike in some other fin types, the caudal fin usually only has one split in it.

- Crown tail: this type of fin, also known as a fringe tail, gets its name from the fact that the rays or thin spines in the fins extend beyond the coloured membrane. This makes them look like a crown.

- Half-moon: the caudal fin is "D" shaped with straight edges and the fin forms an 180° angle to the body. There is also a short-finned version of the half-moon.

- Over-half-moon: in these fish the caudal fin stands at an angle greater than 180°. While they look beautiful, these fish can battle to swim because the fins are so large.

- Rose tail: this is a variation of the half-moon but in the case of the rose tail there is so much fin that it overlaps and looks like the folding petals of a rose.

- Feather tail: these fish look like the rose tail but the edges of the fins are rougher.

- Delta: these fish have a narrower tail spread than the half-moon and the edges are straight.

- Plakat or short-finned fighting style: this is a hybrid variety that creates a short fin and is a cross between the short-finned Betta and the half-moon.

- Fan tail: as the name implies, the tail is shaped like a Chinese fan and has neat edges rather than more irregular or flowing ones.

- Double tail: the dorsal fin is very long and the tailfin splits into two, hence the name.
- Elephant ear: the white pectoral fins are larger than average and are thought to resemble elephant's ears in shape.

- Comb tail: this variety is similar to the crown tail but the tail is not extended as far or as broad so it resembles a comb.

- Spade tail: these fish have wide-based caudal fins that narrow to a point.

6) Betta colours

In the wild the *Betta splendens* is only brightly coloured when agitated (if threatened or during spawning displays for example). Breeders have exploited this ability and the pigments in the cells to make the vibrant colours permanent.

The colours that the Betta is available in range from opaque white (not to be confused with albino specimens) to black. In between there are yellows, oranges, reds, greens, blues and a range of delicate pastel shades. There are also fish that are multi-coloured. In addition, there are some metallic shades including platinum, gold and copper.

What makes the blues, greens and turquoises even more eye-catching is that they have an iridescent quality and almost appear to change colour slightly as the fish moves. This is due to the fact that these colours are created by the refraction of light through a layer of quinine crystals in the skin cells rather than by pigment in these cells.

In addition to the astonishing range of colours, there are different patterns too, including "butterfly" and "marble" patterns.

While colour, fin varieties and patterns have been manipulated very successfully by breeders, there is one variety of *Betta splendens* that eludes them: the true albino. A couple of albino Bettas have occurred spontaneously but they have yet to be bred.

7) Choosing the right Betta fish

Betta fish are suitable for beginners and experienced hobbyists as they are fairly hardy and don't require very tricky tank and water parameters.

Deciding on the right variety or individual fish depends on what you are looking for. If you want more than one *Betta splendens* in the same tank it is better not to get two males, as they will fight. For hobbyists that want to breed these fish then it is, naturally, necessary to get a male and a female. If appearance is the overriding factor then you can simply choose the fish you think is most beautiful in terms of colour and fin and tail types.

8) Myths & misunderstandings about Betta fish

The Betta fish is endangered

There is no arguing with the fact that our rivers and landmasses are increasingly polluted and that this destroys habitats and food supplies. One also can't dispute the fact that some Betta fish are still caught in the wild. Both of these factors pose a threat to these fish.

There are other factors that counterbalance these threats and help to ensure that, for now at least, the Betta fish is not in danger. Firstly, the distribution of these fish in the wild is still fairly large. This means that the numbers in the wild are probably still high.

However, we can't be complacent about any species, so it's really important to continue to have responsible and established captive breeding programs and make sure that people who own *Betta splendens* are educated and committed to caring for their fish.

They are hard to care for

This, too, is not accurate. Firstly, Bettas are no more susceptible to disease or parasites than any other species of fish. However, thanks to their more aggressive nature, they may suffer injuries if males are kept together.

Furthermore, the water and tank parameters or conditions that they require are not as difficult to maintain or as demanding as for some other types of fish.

One does need, though, to take into consideration the fact that males will have to be kept apart. Even females, while less likely to fight, may not always get on well. One may need to separate fish by dividing tank space.

They don't need to be kept in a tank or fed a wide diet

The erroneous beliefs that the *Betta splendens* doesn't need to be housed in a good sized tank or fed on anything other than plant roots have been responsible for the misery and / or death of many of these lovely fish.

They have been, and continue to be, sold in interior décor and other shops as party favours, table centrepieces or decorations. The containers used range from vases to brandy or champagne glasses. The vases sometimes come complete with a plant such as a peace lily that has sent roots out into the water.

No fish can survive in a container that small. While labyrinth fish such as the *Betta splendens* can breathe at the surface they still need oxygenated water. In addition, they won't be able to breathe at the surface as they need to in a vase that has a plant floating on it. These fish will sicken and eventually die.

Similarly, the roots of a plant in the container are not adequate food for Bettas. While the plant matter may sustain them for a short period, the Betta will eventually die a slow and painful death from malnutrition and starvation. They need non-plant based, high protein food too as they, like so many fish, are omnivorous.

Chapter 3: Betta fish behaviour

1) Social behaviour

There are several categories of behaviour that are significant for the hobbyist or aquarist:

- Aggressive behaviour
- Courtship behaviour, and
- Indicators of illness (these will be discussed in detail in a later chapter).

Aggression

The aggression of the *Betta splendens*, especially the males, is one of the characteristics for which these fish are known. As mentioned earlier, this trait was exploited by those who were involved with arranging contests between fighting fish and by the punters who placed bets on the outcome of these fights.

One behavioural indicator of aggression is the activity known as "flaring". The fish puff out their gill covers and this makes them look larger and therefore more intimidating. The aim is to scare off a rival or defend their territory.

When a Betta actually attacks another they will bite each other's fins, tails or even lock mouths. However, it is very unlikely that a fight would result in severe injury, never mind death; the weaker or less aggressive fish will withdraw before that stage is reached.

If one has two male fish that are aggressive one may have to separate them to prevent the stress they will both begin to suffer from. Very aggressive males may even attack their own reflections!

Some females may show aggression too but this is not common. Conversely, not all male Bettas will act with aggression or get into fights.

Courtship

Flaring is also part of courtship, as both the males and females flare in order to attract a mate. Males flare to show strength and females to indicate readiness or interest.

In addition to increasing their size by puffing out their gill covers, there is another signal that is visual rather than behavioural: the females exhibit vertical stripes on their bodies that say they are ready to breed.

Behavioural and other signs of illness

Signs of ill health in fish vary from illness to illness but there are a number of reliable general indicators:

- Paler than usual, even grey in colour
- Loss of, or reduction in, appetite
- Tummy is either swollen or hollow-looking
- Scales are not smooth but raised
- Tail and or fins look different: frayed, closed or stiff
- Reduction in activities such as swimming
- Sores, lumps, spots or white fluffy-looking patches
- Swollen and / or bulging eye or eyes
- Frequently rubs itself on rough surfaces like rocks or gravel
- Gills stay open or partly open or they look red or swollen.

2) Compatibility with other Bettas and other species

Betta fish, especially but not only the males, are aggressive when it comes to defending their territory. They are also more solitary fish and are never found in schools or groups in the wild. These facts must be kept in mind when selecting Bettas and deciding on other fish, if any, for your tank. However, don't believe the story that all Bettas have to be kept on their own.

Hobbyists have successfully kept two female Bettas together or a single male Betta in a tank with fish of other species. You could even try two males together and see how they get on with each other…

If you want a tank or aquarium with a range of fish, including a Betta or two, you should avoid other aggressive species, very small fish that may be attacked or eaten by the Betta, or fish that look similar to *Betta splendens*.

Other species of fish, invertebrates and amphibians that are a good combination with Bettas include the following species:

- Neon / Cardinal and Black Skirt Tetras
- Mollies
- Blue Gourami
- Glass Catfish
- Wild Guppies
- Swordtails
- White Cloud Minnows
- Bristlenose Pleco (a freshwater catfish)
- Otocinclus Catfish
- Corries / Corydoras Catfish
- Rasboras
- Hatchet Fish
- African dwarf frogs
- Ghost Shrimp
- Apple Snails

This list is offered by many retailers and hobbyists but they may not all hit it off with your *Betta splendens*. This may be especially true of Guppies, which can be a little temperamental themselves.

3) Compatibility with other Betta fish

As previously stated, most Bettas don't get on well with other Bettas, especially the males of the species. Generally, females will get on with each other or at least tolerate each other. Fish have personalities so there are exceptions. If Bettas don't get on well they may have to be separated. Generally, though, two bettas is the maximum in a tank or aquarium regardless of whether they are male or female.

4) Bullying of other tank inhabitants

It is not unusual for new arrivals of any species to be chased or even attacked by the fish that are already in residence. As previously indicated, Bettas are aggressive and territorial at the best of times and will probably want to show the newcomer in no uncertain terms that he is not welcome at all or in certain areas of the tank! If this bullying is of concern, there are a few tricks one can try.

The first option is to partition off a section of your aquarium or tank so that you keep the aggressive fish away from the others. You can use any type of barrier that is easy to clean, won't contaminate the water and allows water to pass freely through it. For example, one can use a plastic grid like that used for lighting systems or some kind of plastic mesh.

If the aggression between the fish is not a long-term problem, the aggressor can be placed in a plastic vegetable or pasta strainer or colander. One simply floats it in the tank and it acts as a holding area. Leave the problematic fish in its temporary 'cage' for around 4 hours, by which time it should be safe to reintroduce it into the tank because the new tank inhabitant or inhabitants will have had a chance to adjust and settle in by then.

Both of these options are both inexpensive and easy to manage. Using one or both will greatly reduce the stress experienced by tank inmates and the chances of injury.

Chapter 4: Buying your Betta fish

1) Wild caught versus a Betta fish bred in captivity

It is highly unlikely that hobbyists would buy a Betta caught in the wild because they are drab and have short fins. However, for those individuals who, for some reason, do want a wild-caught specimen, there are factors that must be considered. The general consensus is that Betta bred in captivity offer advantages over ones that have been caught in the wild.

- Captive-bred fish are far less likely to carry disease or parasites. Wild-caught specimens on the other hand often carry parasites of various kinds. Diseases and internal or external parasites threaten the fish's health and can also be passed on to other fish in the tank.

- They are used to people and are even 'pleased' to see people approach the tank because they associate them with food. Fish that are captured in the wild are often frightened and may therefore become more aggressive. This usually passes with time but wild-caught fish are never quite as relaxed around people.

- Captive-bred fish acclimatize to tank life far more easily. Although moving to a new tank is stressful, is it far less so for these fish than for those taken from the wild and placed in a tank.

- In addition, captive-bred fish are used to small spaces, sharing tank space with other fish and species and with artificial fish food. Even so, correct acclimation procedures are essential with any fish, and they will be discussed in detail in a later chapter.

- "Shipping stress" is caused by one or more of the changes and moves that a fish would go through. These include collection, exportation / shipment, importation, placed in a new tank at a wholesaler, transported, rehoused in another tank at a retailer and then moved again once it has been bought by an aquarist who takes it home.

- Captive-bred fish do not go through several of these traumatic changes. Fish bought from on-line retailers usually miss out yet another of these stressful changes.

- Bettas captured in the wild are far more likely to exhibit more aggressive behaviour than captive-bred fish. In the wild, these fish must defend their territory and they will continue to act in this way once in captivity. This can lead to injuries or even deaths if they are placed in tanks with other less aggressive fish.

- With captive bred or tank reared fish one is far more likely to get a young fish as most are sold when they are less than a year old. There is no way of assessing the age of a wild-caught Betta and one could get a fish that is already approaching the end of its lifespan.

- There is mortality with both captive and wild Bettas but this can and should be reduced by ensuring that tank conditions are optimal and by reducing the stress the fish experience. Mortality due to disease and parasites can be hard to avoid.

  The mortality rate with wild caught fish is, not surprisingly, higher than with tank reared fish. As already discussed, these fish are subjected to far more handling and stress and have to make huge adjustments to life in a tank. As mentioned before, they also may already be fairly old.

  Furthermore, both captive bred and wild caught fish will die if they are introduced into a tank without correct acclimation and into a tank environment that is not correct for them. Those who buy Bettas or any other fish have a responsibility to give it or them the correct care and environment.

2) Male and female Betta fish

How one can tell of a fish is male or female

It is not difficult to tell whether a Betta is male or female. There are a few ways one can establish gender:

- ✓ *Size*: As with most species of fish, the males are larger than the females. The difference is not very large but significant enough to be used as a gender-determining factor. In addition, the males are thinner than the females.

- ✓ *Colour*: This can be an indicator of sex but is not always a 100% reliable one. With Bettas, breeders have worked at producing colourful females as well as males. However, the females are less vibrant or vivid in colour.

- ✓ *Fins and tails*: The fins and tails of female Bettas are shorter, smaller and less flowing than those of their male counterparts.

- ✓ *Behaviour*: Male Bettas are aggressive and territorial. The females are far less combative.

- ✓ *Sex organs*: Females have an "egg spot" on the underside of their bodies. This is a small white spot and in some fish it protrudes very slightly. It can be very hard to find on some fish, however.

Some of these indicators are not noticeable until the fish is older or more mature.

3) How to ensure the Betta you want is healthy

While it is not possible to be 100% sure that a *Betta splendens* is free of disease and parasites, there are certain basics that one should check:

- ✓ Colours are bright and vibrant

- ✓ The eyes should be clear and not clouded or opaque or protruding
- ✓ The fins and tail must be spread out, flowing and moving
- ✓ The fish should be active (in other words, swimming with ease, able to change direction etc.)
- ✓ Breathing should be easy and not laboured or erratic and the fish should breathe at both the surface and in the water
- ✓ It should have a healthy appetite
- ✓ The fish should look clean (no blotches, lumps or cysts, or 'scaly' or white patches)
- ✓ The scales should be flat and smooth
- ✓ The fins should not have ragged edges and look discoloured (keep in mind that some Betta fin and tail types look 'ragged' and should not be mistaken for signs of disease)
- ✓ There should be no spots or white patches inside the mouth
- ✓ The gills should be clear and not very red or swollen
- ✓ There should be no sign of parasites
- ✓ The tummy should not look bloated or concave / too thin.

Chapter 5: What you need to buy for your Betta fish

1) Essential basic equipment & supplies

While this is not necessarily an exhaustive list, it does give an indication of the basic items or supplies required in order to set up a tank or aquarium for Betta fish.

- Tank or aquarium (minimum 2 gallons / 7.5 liters)
- Substrate for the bottom of the tank or aquarium
- Décor (rocks, plants etc.)
- Filter
- Thermometer
- Heater
- Full spectrum light
- Aquarium salt
- Water test kit
- Water conditioner to remove chlorine and heavy metals from water
- Biological conditioner that deals with harmful substances such as nitrates and ammonia
- Suitably sized soft and flexible net
- Protein skimmer
- Appropriate food (frozen and dried).

Investing in a book or two about aquariums generally and / or *Betta splendens* specifically is also recommended. The more you, as a tank and Betta owner, know the easier your life will be and the happier and healthier your fish will be!

2) The aquarium or tank

It is suggested that Bettas need an aquarium that holds an absolute minimum of 2 gallons or 9.1 litres (UK) or 7.5 litres (US). Some aquarists, however, insist that a 10 gallon or 45.5 litre (UK) or 37.5 litre (US) tank is the minimum capacity. In Germany, the minimum prescribed by law is 13 gallons or 59 litres (UK) or 49 litres (US).

Tanks must also provide space that can accommodate the décor items fish need such as rocks and plants. Bettas and other fish need space for swimming too.

Ironically, smaller tanks are far more work for the aquarist. The reason for this is that toxins build up much faster in a smaller tank or aquarium than they do in a large one. Toxins such as nitrates or ammonia have very negative effects on water quality.

This in turn has detrimental and potentially serious effects on the health of the fish and other species in the tank. It also leads to algae growth, which is both unhealthy and ugly to look at. A good filtration system is essential but there is no substitute for regular water changes!

Chapter 6: Setting up the aquarium

Setting up an aquarium takes time and effort. However, this initial investment is well worth it as it ensures a tank that is pleasing to look at and – more importantly – provides the right environment to keep your Bettas and any tank mates they may have happy and healthy.

No step in the process should therefore be left out. There are, broadly speaking, 6 stages that one should go through in setting up a tank or aquarium:

1) Preparing the water for the aquarium or tank

This stage of the process involves several steps that should be carried out several days before fish are introduced into the water:

- Install the water filtration system
- Treat the water you will use by reverse osmosis, if possible
- Add a liquid de-chlorinator if you are using city water
- Add aquarium salt mix
- Check the salt or salinity levels using a hydrometer
- Adjust salt levels as necessary
- Install and set a heater to the appropriate temperature
- Let the tank run for several days
- Monitor water quality and temperature regularly to ensure that the equipment is working as it should.

Some of these aspects, specifications and items of equipment will be discussed again in a later section of the book.

2) Building the aquarium or tank substrate

If stage 1 has been successful, one can then build the substrate or what is referred to as the aquarium or tank's foundation. More simply put, the substrate is the material used to line or cover the base or bottom of the tank.

A substrate is important not only in terms of aesthetics but also because of the impact it can have on the health of the tank's occupants and the ease with which the tank can be kept clean. The type you select will also be affected by whether or not you want to grow live plants in it.

There are four aspects of a substrate that should be considered:

1. *Impact on the fish and other tank occupants*: Some substrates can affect the well being of fish, snails, etc. For instance, there are substrates that have sharp edges, which can cause injuries, or particles so small they can get into mouths, eyes and gills and cause irritation.

2. *Effects on the water*: There are substrates that can affect water parameters such as pH or acidity levels. As mentioned in section 1 above, substrates that trap waste products will negatively affect the overall quality of water.

3. *Colour*: This is the least crucial decision as colour is primarily a personal choice based on what you like. Whether you want bright or neutral colours, there is a substrate for you!

   The only important consideration is that very bright or highly reflective substrate can frighten or dazzle fish. It is also a good idea to opt for a colour that will show the occupants of your tank to their best advantage. Keep in mind that a very dark tank will also seem smaller.

4. *Particle size*: Substrates come in particles as small as grains of sand to as large as pieces of rock or stone. Both extremes can cause problems.

Waste and uneaten food particles can build up under and between stones and rocks, which severely affects water quality. Sand, on the other hand, can become compacted and may even release toxic substances such as hydrogen sulphide. In addition, sand is hard to clean.

A further option is no substrate at all! This might not look at all attractive but it is very easy to clean. However, most aquarists state that this is only a good option in quarantine and hospital tanks or ones in which fry or baby fish are being reared. The standard substrates are:

- *Gravel* of various colours is the most popular choice for tanks, aquariums and even fish bowls that contain substrate. Here again one can select from a range of gravel particle sizes. It is better, for reasons discussed earlier, not to get gravel with either very large or very small pieces.

  Gravel that does not have sharp edges should be chosen, especially if you have fish that dig in the substrate or spend time on it such as catfish, as they will be hurt.

- *Sand* is also often used as a substrate. It can look lovely and is kinder to fish with sensitive skin or mouthparts but it is also harder to clean and one can loose a lot of it each time one vacuums up dirt. One can buy replacement sand regularly or use a more gentle siphoning action to try to overcome this problem.

  The other considerations with sand are that you can't use an under-substrate filter and that sand particles can get into filters and block them. Sand also shows dirt and waste much faster than gravel does. A further disadvantage is that sand often becomes compacted and this makes it hard for plants to take root or grow.

- A less common type of substrate is *crushed coral*. This should be used with caution as it raises water pH and it can be rough or have jagged edges. It should especially be used with caution in fresh water tanks and aquariums.

In terms of *plants*, the substrate that you choose must allow the plants to take root and grow. It must also be able to support the plants so that they do not become uprooted or float free. Plants will also need to draw nutrients from the environment they live in.

3) Placing and arranging rocks or stones

Rocks and stones are one of the most important décor items as they create hiding places for fish and make a tank look far more interesting.

The number and size of rocks and stones must be dictated by the size of the aquarium. Some hobbyists use the following guideline: 1 to 1.5 pounds of rock or stone or 450 to 680 grams per gallon or 3.75 US or 4.55 UK litres.

When arranging the rocks in an aquarium or tank one should take the time and trouble to do so in such a way that one:

- ✓ Builds caves – as many as possible – for fish to hide in
- ✓ Allows fish and other tank inhabitants to move around freely
- ✓ Permits the water to circulate freely between the rocks and throughout the tank
- ✓ Allows free and easy access to tank equipment.

4) Plants

The choices when it comes to plants are simple: plants or no plants and, if you want plants, should they be real or fake (silk or plastic).

There are advantages to plastic plants because they don't need nutrients or light and there is no need to trim or otherwise care for them. The disadvantages, in addition to the fact that they usually look like plastic, are that they don't neutralise harmful ammonia in the water or release the oxygen the tank inhabitants need.

Plastic also poses a risk to fish as the edges of the leaves can be sharp and can catch on fins.

Live plants look much better… if they are healthy and cared for. To thrive they need a supportive type of substrate that they can grow in, nutrients, good light, Co2 supplements and the odd trim.

In exchange for this and in addition to looking good, live plants provide good cover for tank inhabitants, neutralise ammonia and give off oxygen.

5) Lighting and items to combat algae in the tank

Once you have placed the rocks and plants and run the tank or aquarium to make sure that the temperature is correct and constant, the next step is to add the lighting.

Ideally, an aquarium or tank lighting system should be placed on a timer so that even if you are not home there will be light for the necessary number of hours each day. Bettas don't require a great deal of light. However, other fish or the invertebrates in the tank or aquarium might.

After light has been introduced to the tank there will be a significant amount of algae growth or what is known as algae bloom. An aquarist wants to avoid this as it impacts negatively on water quality, the health of the creatures in the aquarium, the way the tank looks, visibility and work load for the tank owner who will have to clean the tank.

The way to avoid algae bloom is by using what is called an algae attack pack. These packs are a natural way of controlling algae growth and maintaining clear, good quality water. An algae attack pack does not contain chemicals, minerals or any artificial substances.

Depending on the type of pack you buy you will be introducing a number of water creatures into the tank that will feed off the algae. Catfish, which tend to get on well with *Betta splendens*, also help with algae control.

The algae attack pack is simply added to the aquarium just before the lights are put on for the first time. Each pack gives details of the acclimation or acclimatisation process required. The filtration system in your tank will then have to adjust to accommodate the new residents of your aquarium.

When the algae pack creatures, for example fresh-water snails, have been in the tank for a few days you need to test the water again, focussing on nitrite and ammonia levels as these will be affected by the new arrivals.

Once the levels of these two toxins have reached 0 you can begin the exciting process of introducing your Bettas and other fish and invertebrates!

6) Introducing fish and invertebrates to the aquarium

Before you can take this step you need to go through this checklist:

- ✓ You have cleaned any rocks or stones you have using fresh, clean water (no soap should be used)
- ✓ You have arranged the rocks in such as way as to create caves and allow space for swimming and free water flow
- ✓ The nitrite and ammonia levels in the tank are at zero and remain that way
- ✓ The temperature remains correct and constant
- ✓ The salinity levels are correct and constant
- ✓ The lighting and filtration systems are working correctly
- ✓ You have installed an algae attack pack that has acclimated
- ✓ There is no algae bloom

And, importantly:

- ✓ You have done research on the various fish and invertebrate species
- ✓ You have learnt all you can about general tank care
- ✓ You have made sure that the fish you want to place in your aquarium with your *Betta splendens* are compatible!

If you can tick off each of these items you are ready to begin stocking your tank!

However, there are a few rules that govern this exciting and fun stage of setting up a tank or aquarium:

- It is very important that you introduce stock gradually so that the various filtration systems – mechanical and biological – can adjust to each new batch of inhabitants.
- Begin with the fish and other species that are docile and non-aggressive or territorial. They need a chance to settle and establish themselves before the arrival of the more assertive species.

  It is suggested that they should be left in the tank for several weeks before larger or more aggressive species are introduced.

In terms of how many fish one can have in a tank or aquarium there is a guideline rather than a hard and fast rule because it depends on several factors including the species involved and their requirements and temperaments. Generally, it is thought that one can have 0.5 inches or 1.25 centimetres of adult or fully grown fish for every gallon or 3.7 US or 4.5 litres UK of water in the tank.

7) Air and water flow systems

The majority of the oxygen that is in tank or aquarium water is dissolved oxygen from the surface of the water. The water works the same way our bodies do because oxygen is taken in and carbon dioxide and other toxic or unwanted gasses are released.

If you only have *Betta splendens* in your tank or aquarium you will not need an air pump and system because, like all labyrinth fish, they will get all the oxygen they need from the surface and the water. However, if you have other creatures in the tank, the water surface will supply much but not all the oxygen they need and you will have to get some kind of air system.

There is a wide range of these devices available currently and you will need to select one based on the size of your aquarium or tank, the needs of the fish and so forth in it, and your budget. It's a good idea to get advice from a reliable and honest dealer as it can become confusing. The main types of air systems one can get are:

- Under-gravel bubble systems
- Air stones.

Both are driven by electrical air pumps. In terms of water flow or circulation, aquarists often use a combination of:

- Powerheads
- Wave-makers
- Oscillators.

Under-gravel filters

As the name suggests, these fairly thin and flat filters are placed under the gravel or sand at the bottom of a tank or aquarium when you are setting it up. While they are actually there to aid with filtration and water quality, they also release air bubbles, which move the water up to the surface.

This helps with the exchange of various gasses into and out of the water. Other advantages of these filters are that the bubbles that are released are attractive and these items of equipment are relatively inexpensive.

On the down side some tank owners find the constant sound made by the bubbles irritating. Others find it soothing…

Air stones

Air stones are very popular with a lot of aquarists. One can either buy or even make an air stone. The name is a little deceptive in that these items are not necessarily stone. They could be made of wood, glass or ceramic. They are connected to a hose through which air, generated by an air pump, flows.

Although they are aesthetically appealing, are inexpensive, release air bubbles that move water up to the surface and so enable the exchange of gasses, there are disadvantages too.

The primary disadvantage of air stones is that they are not able to move a large volume of water quickly because they simply don't have the power. This means they are not very efficient and are totally inadequate for larger tanks.

The water in an aquarium should ideally move both horizontally and upwards or vertically. This ensures that all the water in the tank is properly circulated. Air stones can't achieve this either. Other problems and drawbacks include:

- The air flow can be irregular and the air pressure is often too low because the pump is inadequate for the size or depth of the tank or the pipe is too long
- They clog up and the air flow diminishes further or stops
- The pipe running to the stone can become squashed or bent and this will also negatively affect or even stop air flow
- They need to be replaced much more often than other types as they become worn out or blocked

However, they are an important part of protein skimming or foam fractionating in a tank (more on this later).

Powerheads

A Powerhead is an electrical unit that can be safely submerged in water.

This is thanks to the fact that they are sealed. They can be positioned on the bottom of a tank or attached to the sides. While Powerheads are used to run or power various pieces of equipment in an aquarium such as various types of filters, protein skimmers and air pumps, they are also ideal for water circulation. Naturally, the larger the tank, the more Powerheads one must use.

The basic advantages they offer an aquarist are that they are very effective, economical in terms of power consumption and they are fairly inexpensive. They make the tank a healthier environment for all the inhabitants because of the strength and consistency of the water flow they generate. The associated benefits include:

- Greatly improved water quality
- Improved oxygenation, which promotes the health of the tank's occupants
- Reduced detritus in the tank by improving filtration
- Algae growth is deterred or significantly reduced
- Food brought to stationary creatures in the tank
- The tank inhabitants are stimulated to move and so get exercise, which improves their health.

All of these are due to one factor: the strong water circulation throughout the tank or aquarium generated by Powerheads.

While there is no doubt that buying a Powerhead is an excellent investment, it is also necessary to place them with care and caution. For instance, some fish and other tank occupants thrive in a strong current while others will not flourish at all. This means the Powerhead must be placed where it will not adversely affect anything in the tank.

There is a confusing array of Powerheads on the market. Here are some tips to guide you in terms of choosing a suitable and reliable Powerhead for your aquarium or tank:

- ✓ Spend a little more money to buy a brand name Powerhead such as one manufactured by Hagen or Marineland for example. If you do so you can rest assured that you are getting a reliable product that is tested and should last.

  'Budget' versions may cost less initially but they are far more likely to burn out.

- ✓ You need to invest in a Powerhead that you can get parts for easily if you need them. It also helps if the unit can be opened and disassembled and then reassembled easily for repair purposes.

- ✓ The interior may need cleaning from time to time and this is another reason why it should be a unit that can be opened with ease. If you can't clean the interior regularly or as necessary it may burn out if it becomes clogged.

- ✓ A good Powerhead will be moisture proof and, preferably, epoxy sealed. This will prevent both water getting in and electricity leaking out!

- ✓ Buy a model that has a screen of some kind that will prevent any of the fish or invertebrates in your tank accidentally being sucked into the intake hole of the Powerhead. Just make sure the holes in the screen are not too small because they will clog up with dirt very quickly. This in turn will reduce the water intake, which can lead to the motor becoming overheated or even burning out.

- ✓ If possible, select a Powerhead that allows you to adjust the water rate. This will mean that you can reduce or increase the rate of flow (or even reverse it) depending on the needs of your tank and its inhabitants.

- ✓ As an optional extra you could purchase a directional flow diffuser that fits onto the Powerhead. This will enable you to direct the water flow in your tank with even greater accuracy and care.

Once you have selected the model you want you need to decide how many Powerheads you need and where you will place it or them in your tank. The size of your aquarium is the most significant factor.

If you have a tank that is 20 gallons (91 litres UK or 76 litres US) or less you have two options: a single large Powerhead or two less powerful ones that can be placed at either end of the tank. Medium to large tanks will need more units and more powerful ones. Often a smaller unit is placed at each corner.

The bottom line is that you need as many Powerheads as it will take to create the amount of water circulation or flow that your tank requires in order to maintain good water quality.

The finally important aspect of Powerheads is flow rates. These will also depend on whether you have a tank that only contains fish or a reef tank as one would have with Betta fish.

Most experienced hobbyists believe that the water in the tank should be turned over, or circulated throughout the tank, between 6 and 10 times an hour. A few aquarists say that reef tanks should have a flow of 15 to 20 times an hour.

What is essential is that a balance is struck between:

- Circulating the water so that it and the tank inhabitants get all the benefits that it brings

- Not making fish swim against currents constantly as this will exhaust them, or creating such strong and constant currents that invertebrates are damaged or harmed.

Wave makers and Oscillators

Wave makers are connected to controlling devices that turn the Powerheads on and off at set and regular intervals. This creates a variable current and waves. Oscillators, on the other hand, create random currents by rotating the Powerhead rather than turning it on and off.

8) Protein Skimmers

In this context "protein" refers to the muck that floats around in the water. It consists of bits of uneaten food and waste matter of various kinds. This must be removed from the water and this is achieved through skimming or, to use the correct technical term, the process of "foam fractionating". This sounds complicated and impressive but it isn't. Skimming is quite simply using water bubbles to remove protein molecules from the water.

What happens is that as the column or columns of air bubbles rise from the floor of the tank or aquarium, the molecules of protein attach themselves to the surface of the bubbles. These waste products rise to the surface of the water, where they are collected in a container.

The trick to successful skimming is that there must be a large number of bubbles because the more bubbles there are the more protein will be collected. In addition, the longer the bubble column is the better as this gives the bubbles more time to attract protein molecules to them. Furthermore, the smaller the bubble the more slowly it rises and the more effectively it gathers protein molecules.

In summary, bubble columns should:

- ✓ Contain a lot of bubbles
- ✓ Be as long as possible
- ✓ Consist of small bubbles or at least some small bubbles.

There are two types of skimming apparatus: co-current and counter-current.

One can have a vertical column of bubbles. These bubbles follow their natural tendency to rise to the surface. When they reach the surface of the water they burst and leave the proteins behind, often in the form of foam. Skimmers like this that use vertical bubble columns are known as co-current skimmers.

Other skimmers, called counter-current skimmers, force the bubbles downwards through the water or even sideways. Again, this is in order to keep the bubbles in the water for as long as possible so that they collect the optimal amount of protein.

The air that is used to create the bubbles is usually sent into the skimmer by means of a diffuser such as an air stone or an air pump.

What to look for in a Protein Skimmer

As with other pieces of tank equipment, there is a wide range of skimmers from which to choose. There are some things that you should look for in a protein skimmer or a foam fractionating system:

- Look for a skimmer that is easy to maintain. You don't want a model that is difficult to work with so that you battle to remove, for instance, the collection container.
- The skimmer should be adjustable so that you can change and manage the water flow in the skimmer's reaction chamber. A manufacturer's claim that "No adjustments are needed" often actually translates as "No adjustments are possible"!
- You need to know where you are going to put the skimmer in your tank or aquarium. That will help you decide which model to get as some, for instance, are placed in the tank and others on it.

As with any aspect of a tank or aquarium's equipment, don't ever be reluctant or afraid to ask for information and advice!

9) Heating / Temperature control

Bettas, like all fish, are cold blooded. This means that they are not able, as we are able, to raise or lower their body temperature in response to changes in their environment. It is therefore the tank owner's responsibility to provide heat and maintain the correct temperature for the creatures in the tank.

Betta splendens are hardy and can cope with a fairly wide temperature range. However, the consensus is that ideally the water temperature must be between 75 and 80° Fahrenheit or 24 and 27° Celsius.

If the water temperature is lower than 75 or 27 degrees it will damage a Betta's immune system and this will make it more susceptible to disease. Conversely, water that is too warm can cause fish to age faster as their metabolism is accelerated to an unhealthy degree.

Types of heating units

As with all the other items for your tank you will be faced with a choice when it comes to buying a heater for it. There are three options:

- *Heating cable systems*: These are placed under the substrate of the tank and are connected to an electronic controlling unit. These systems are often used for fresh water tanks.

  The primary advantage of cable heating systems is that they distribute heat very evenly throughout the tank. This is mainly due to the fact that heat rises.

  However, there is a major drawback with them: if the system goes wrong and must be repaired or replaced you will have to remove everything from the tank before you can remove it from under the substrate!

- *Submersible heaters*: These heaters can be mounted from the side of a tank or placed on the substrate. Because they are fully submerged in the water they heat the water very effectively. They are also easy to lift out if necessary.

- *Hang-on-tank heaters*: These, as the name implies, hang on the interior of the tank. They are only partly submerged beneath the water line. While they, too, are easy to remove if needs be, they are not efficient heaters because they are not fully submerged.

Words of caution

If you opt for either a submersible or a hang-on heater, it is a good idea to have more than one so you have one in reserve. This way, if the heater malfunctions or breaks down you have a backup unit available. Sometimes one doesn't have time to get a new one before the temperature in the tank changes significantly...with potentially fatal results.

If you have a medium or large aquarium you will need more than one heater anyway in order to maintain constant temperatures throughout the tank. In this situation too, you should have a heating unit in reserve.

Other factors to consider

When selecting and installing a heating unit or units you need to keep in mind that it or they won't be the only source of heat. Some heat will be given off by lights, other tank equipment such as Powerheads, heating sources in the room such as vents or central heating units and even the seasonal temperature extremes in your area that make a difference to the ambient temperature in the room.

All of these heat sources and temperature factors will affect the temperature in the tank. This, in turn, will impact on your decision about the size heater your aquarium will need. Fortunately, there is a rule of thumb guideline used by aquarists that will be of help: you need to use 2.5 – 5 watts per gallon (3.75 US or 4.55 UK litres) of water. Once you have calculated how many watts your tank will need, you can work out the heater size and the number you will need.

How to deal with an overheating crisis

The inhabitants of a tank or aquarium are very susceptible to changes in water temperature. Water that becomes too warm is fatal even faster than water that has become too cool. Tank owners who battle the most with this are those in very hot climates. However, it can affect other aquarists too.

Regardless of the reason for it, an overheating problem must be resolved as fast as possible. There are things that can be done quickly and without special equipment:

- *Open or remove covers or hoods*: A cover or hood on a tank or aquarium traps heat. If the cover on your tank is hinged, you need to open it and leave it open until the crisis has passed. If there is a loose lid on your aquarium you need to remove it and leave it off for as long as necessary.

  In fact, consider not putting it back because using a hood or cover is not generally recommended because they reduce aeration, lower oxygen levels and increase carbon dioxide levels.

- *Fans*: Place small fans near the tank or clip-on fans on the sides or top of the tank. The fans should be directed in such a way that the air flows across the top of the water. The flow of air should be strong but not so much so that it causes any significant surface disturbance.

- *Adjust the lighting in the tank*: As mentioned earlier, lights generate heat. Different types of lighting give off varying amounts of heat. Fluorescent lights produce the least amount of heat and metal provides the most.

  An easy way to reduce heat, therefore, is to have 'hot' lights on for fewer hours each day or, alternatively, only have the fluorescents on. You could do this for up to 2 days without impacting negatively on the tank's inhabitants.

- *Use ice*: This is also not a complex solution but it is both effective and quick. It's a good idea to keep a few ice packs in the freezer in case they are needed. You need to begin by removing some of the water from your tank because the water level will rise when you introduce the ice.

  You can use plastic bottles that you filled with water and froze or sealed bags that contain ice cubes. Either type can be placed into the tank where they will float and slowly melt, lowing the water temperature as they do so.

- *Buy or make a chiller*: You can buy a chiller from a retailer if you wish to do so. Other and more experienced aquarists make their own chillers using ice, an ice chest, a water pump and plastic tubes. There are a number of plans and ideas for do-it-yourself chillers available on the Internet.

With any and all of these methods it is essential to monitor the temperature regularly. The last thing one wants is for the water to go from too hot to too cold! In order to monitor it accurately you will require an accurate thermometer of some kind.

10) Thermometers

As with other pieces of equipment, thermometers are no different in that the aquarist is spoiled for choice. You can get one that gives readings in either Fahrenheit or Celsius or both. While there are many kinds of thermometer, they all do the same job. This can make selecting one harder. What is helpful is to look at the pros and cons of each type.

- *Floating thermometers*: This is perhaps the most widely known and earliest kind. They are inexpensive, easy to read, compact, and can either be left to float around freely or be attached to the side of the tank by means of a plastic suction cup.

The downside is that the suction cups wear out and must be replaced regularly or are not effective and don't adhere properly. If the thermometer is free floating, it can bang into the glass sides of the tank and break as these thermometers are also made of glass and you have to look for it each time you want to take a reading. In addition, the numbering is small and can be hard to read.

- *Magnetic thermometers*: These thermometers offer a great deal. They are easy to attach because the thermometer is positioned against the glass on the inside of the tank and the magnet is placed opposite it on the outside of the tank. They are held firmly in place, have easy to read numbers, a broad temperature range and they don't corrode.

  The only disadvantage is that the white plastic casing is not attractive and makes these thermometers highly visible.

- *Stainless steel thermometers*: These, too, are inexpensive types of thermometer and they are usually just mounted to the edge of the tank. Because they are made of stainless steel, they don't corrode or rust. They are easier to read than the smaller, glass thermometers.

  However, because they are fairly large and shiny, they can look unattractive. They also sink if they are dropped or knocked off the aquarium rim.

- *Standing thermometers*: These are compact, affordable and easy to read. They are weighted so they sink to the bottom but remain vertical. However, they come with a host of drawbacks.

  They have a tendency to move around in the currents and can bang against hard surfaces such as rocks or the sides of the aquarium. This makes these thermometers susceptible to breakage. They can also be hard to spot because they move and hard to read as they may be behind or against something.

- *Stick-on Liquid Crystal Display (LCD) thermometers*: These are the easiest thermometer type to install as you just peel off the backing and stick it onto the outside of the tank. Other advantages are that they are low cost and available in a range of sizes and various temperature ranges.

  However, the lamination may separate over time and they can be difficult to read.

- *Remote Sensor Digital thermometers*: Hardly surprisingly, these thermometers are not as inexpensive as others, but they are still not too costly. The advantages include their compact size, the fact that they are easy to read and that the LED display is placed on the outside of the tank or near the tank. A sensor cord runs from the display into the water and this is in part why these thermometers also have some disadvantages.

  The LCD is attached by means of suction cups, which are not always effective and will need replacing. The length of the sensor cord dictates where the LCD can be placed. In addition, the batteries that power the thermometer will need periodic replacing.

- *Submersible LCD digital thermometers*: This kind of thermometer has a great deal in its favour: they are compact, fixed in place, have an easy to read LCD display and they are wireless and fully submersible.

  They are attached by means of suction cups, which can be problematic and will need to be replaced, as will the batteries that power the thermometer.

- *Temperature Alert Remote Sensor digital thermometers*: These thermometers cost a little more than most others but they are compact and easy to read thanks to the LED display.

The biggest selling point is the fact that these thermometers include automatic temperature setting high / low alarms which can be extremely useful.

The length of the sensor cord will limit where the LCD can be placed and the cord is visible. The batteries will of course require periodic replacing. These thermometers are made in either Fahrenheit or Celsius so you need to check that before buying one.

If you feel confused or simply overwhelmed by the range of types of thermometer available, you can find more information and advice online or from a retailer who is familiar with aquariums and the equipment that is necessary for them.

11) UV Sterilisers

An Ultraviolet or UV Steriliser is a nice-to-have but not essential piece of tank equipment. It is used to stop free-floating microorganisms from spreading in a tank or aquarium. This, in turn, serves to control infections and cross-infections between fish, invertebrates and corals. It does so by using UV light to kill these free-floating microorganisms.

It should be noted that they have no effect on microorganisms etc. that are already in or on the creatures in the tank. What is essential is that the UV steriliser is installed and operated correctly!

These sterilisers work by exposing the water that flows through them to UV light from their bulbs. The wavelength of the light is about 254 nanometres or 2537 Angstroms and this irradiates the water as it passes through the steriliser. The effect on bacteria and algae is to mutate its DNA, which in turn prevents them from multiplying or growing.

These sterilisers, if properly used, are said to be effective against algae, bacteria, parasitic protozoa and viruses. The larger the organism is, the higher the required dose of UV will be. For instance, algae must be exposed to far higher doses than a virus has to be.

A UV Steriliser will produce different amounts of light depending on the wattage of the bulb: the higher the wattage the more UV light. It's important to remember, though, that these bulbs degrade with age and must be replaced every 6 months or so.

There are several factors that impact on the effectiveness of a UV Steriliser that should be kept in mind:

- UV light is far less effective at sterilizing water that is murky or dirty. The UV Steriliser must therefore be placed after the filters so that the water is as clear as it can be.

- The UV lamp must be kept clean because, if it becomes covered by a film or layer of deposits of some sort, it will not give off as much UV as possible.

- UV can only penetrate 5 millimetres (a mere 13/64 inch) into water. This means that the lamp must be very close to the water.

- Not surprisingly, the longer the water is exposed to UV, the more microorganisms will be killed. The length of time the water is exposed is determined by the flow rate: the slower the flow the longer the exposure. Using a long bulb will also increase the exposure period.

- Temperature is a further variable that plays a role because UV is optimally produced in warmer temperatures (104 to 110° Fahrenheit or 40 to 43° Celsius). Using a sleeve around the bulb can help to insulate the bulb against water in the aquarium.

While a UV Steriliser certainly offers very significant benefits, they do have a downside:

- They are of no use against any of the disease-causing microorganisms that are not free swimming and against string algae.

- UV can also destroy beneficial bacteria that live in substances such as substrate.

- UV light can destroy the properties of some medications that are in the water. In order to prevent this "denaturing" of medication, the UV should be switched off until the treatment is completed.

- They can cause a rise in water temperature and a chiller may have to be used to counteract this.

It is also important to keep in mind that they don't replace filters and good water quality parameter controls. As previously mentioned, UV is a nice-to-have extra form of protection.

Chapter 7: Water & other parameters

1) pH levels

Maintaining the correct pH level is a very important part of caring for a tank and keeping fish healthy. Power of Hydrogen, or pH, is the measure that tells one if something is acidic or alkaline. A pH reading of 7 is the neutral border between the two. Readings below 7 indicate acidity and those above 7 are alkaline.

Betta splendens are not very susceptible to pH-related problems, as they can tolerate levels between 6.5 and 8. In other words, the water can be slightly acidic, neutral or even slightly alkaline and a Betta will still be happy. However, you may need to be more precise within this range, depending on what your Betta's tank mates require in terms of pH.

Acids can be caused by several things in a tank or aquarium: acids created by waste in the tank that is not effectively removed by filtration and protein skimming, too much carbon dioxide (CO_2) because of poor water circulation and gas exchanges and, finally, nitric acid can be released by rocks that were not properly cleaned and still house microorganisms. All of these build up in the water and drop the pH level dangerously if they are not dealt with.

Freshwater and the oceans and seas have a way of combating all of these acids as they contain what are called "buffers". These consist of various chemicals including hydroxide, calcium, carbonate, bicarbonate and borate. They slow down the drop in pH levels. In order to deal effectively with acidity in a tank, an aquarist must make use of the same buffers.

Ways to avoid pH problems in your tank

The best way to avoid pH problems is to do regular partial water changes - which restore the buffers - and to make sure the tank stays free of the factors that release acids into the water.

One can also invest in a piece of equipment called a “doser”. This item will automatically introduce a range of supplements and trace elements, including buffers, into the water. Calcium reactors are also an option to deal with severe or frequent problems with pH levels. They are costly, though.

Ways to combat pH problems in your tank

If you already have a pH problem in your tank, you need to deal with it quickly and effectively or you run the risk of losing your tank’s inhabitants. The most common options are:

- ✓ If the pH is too low you can add either a pH increaser that you can buy at a retailer or you can add bicarbonate of soda, also known as baking soda.
- ✓ If the pH is too high, home remedies to reduce it include adding small amounts of lemon juice or vinegar to the water. Alternatively, you could buy a commercial pH reduction product.

Many aquarists believe that the three most important aspects are water temperature, pH levels and water quality.

2) Phosphate and Calcium

Phosphate (PO4)

Phosphate (PO4) is a compound of Phosphorous (P). The reason why phosphate levels are of such concern to aquarists is because these compounds are the main source of food or nutrition for various types of algae. So, if there are too many phosphates in a tank, there will be significant algae blooms.

Phosphates are caused by several factors but the most common ones are the use of unfiltered tap water in the tank either as top-up water or to make up aquarium salt mixes and substances put into the tank such as foods and activated carbon in filters.

For this reason, it is strongly suggested that you check ingredient lists on all products so you make sure you are not introducing phosphates or other unwanted compounds or trace elements such as nitrates, for example. There are several things you can do to prevent phosphate build-up and to correct the level if it gets too high.

The first preventative measure is regular tank maintenance. If you perform regular water changes with good quality water you will go a long way to controlling unwanted trace elements and compounds such as phosphates and nitrates. Routine and frequent tests are also necessary because one can't assume that these elements are controlled thanks to the water changes.

If the phosphate levels in your aquarium are too high you can:

- ✓ Use commercial and easily available products that are designed to remove phosphates from tanks and aquariums. There is a range of these products on the market.

  No matter which product one uses, it is essential that they are changed and replenished regularly. If they aren't, they will become saturated with the compounds they have absorbed and will no longer work.

- ✓ Phosphate levels are also reduced if you add a limewater or *kalkwasser* (KW) solution to the water. Limewater is essentially a diluted form of calcium hydroxide, which is believed to effectively remove phosphate because it contains very high levels of calcium.

- ✓ The Vodka Method also removes phosphates (and nitrates) but only when used with a protein skimmer. As the name implies, one adds a small amount of Vodka, or ethanol, to the tank water.

Calcium (Ca)

This is relevant if you have molluscs in your tank because without calcium molluscs, like snails, simply can't grow and survive. These life forms extract calcium from the water and use calcium carbonate to build their skeletal structures. There is a complication, though: calcium hardens water, which is bad for *Betta splendens*!

Fortunately, snails can be fed calcium in the form of algae sticks, which are dropped into the water, sink to the bottom and provide the protein snails need without affecting the water. Spinach can also be fed to snails, as it is also a good source of calcium.

3) The Vodka treatment

It was very briefly mentioned earlier but this cost-effective remedy to reduce both nitrate and phosphate levels in a tank or aquarium justifies closer inspection. Although there are some aquarists that are very sceptical, others believe that using Vodka is effective. More accurately, one uses alcohol or 95% ethanol rather than Vodka.

Why this method works seems to be due to the fact that alcohol contains inorganic carbon. This type of carbon boosts the growth of bacteria in the water. These bacteria work with the aquarist because they actually incorporate or 'feed' on the phosphates and nitrates in the tank. The bacteria in turn are removed when protein skimming occurs.

The Vodka treatment is usually administered each day for three days and involves very, very small quantities. For example, if you had a 50 gallon tank (189 litres US or 227 litres UK) you would add 5 drops of 80% alcohol per day. This translates to 0.25 millilitres or an insanely small 0.0168 fluid ounces!

Chapter 8: Introducing Bettas and other creatures into the tank

After one has bought a *Betta splendens* or two and other fish and tank mates, one can't just put them into the tank no matter how carefully it has been set up and prepared. Why? All the creatures you acquire will have been in water that will have different pH levels and temperatures to the water in your aquarium.

Water-dwellers of various kinds are sensitive to these factors. It is essential that they get used to the changes and differences gradually. This is the purpose of the process called ***acclimation***.

There are a couple of methods one can use. Regardless of which method you opt for, the golden rule with acclimation is not to rush the process. Both methods begin with these steps:

A. Turn off the light or lights in the tank and dim the lights in the room where you will open the box or container the creatures are in. Harsh or bright light and sudden exposure to light is very traumatic and will cause stress.

B. Place the still-sealed bag in the water in your aquarium. After 15 to 20 minutes the water inside the bag will have slowly adjusted to the temperature of the water in the tank. By keeping the bag sealed you ensure that the level of dissolved oxygen in the water in the bag stays high.

The float method

Once you have completed steps A and B above, and have elected to go with the float method, you need to:

1. Cut the bag open just below the metal clip that seals it. Roll the edge of the bag down about 1 inch or 2.5 centimetres so that you create an air pocket in the rolled up section. This air should be enough to keep the bag afloat.

2. Carefully and slowly add a ½ cup of water from your tank or aquarium to the water in the shipping bag. Continue to add a further ½ cup every 4 or 5 minutes until the shipping bag is full.

3. Remove the bag from the water and drain 50% of the water, being careful not to disturb the occupants of the bag.

4. Float the bag in the aquarium again and repeat step 2 until the bag is full once more.

5. Use a suitable net to carefully catch the creature or creatures in the shipping bag and release it / them into the aquarium.

6. Remove the floating shipping bag from the tank and discard the water. It's important that you don't ever place the rest of the water into your tank or aquarium.

The drip method

The drip method is considered to be the preferable one for certain creatures including shrimp. In other words, more sensitive creatures should be acclimatised using this method rather than the float method. The drip method does, however, require additional equipment in the form of air tubing and a bucket or buckets.

The bucket you use must be one that is only used for tank water to prevent possible contamination by, for instance, household cleaning products. Fish should be placed in one bucket and molluscs etc. in a separate one during acclimation. In addition, the tank owner must be involved throughout the process because progress must be monitored constantly.

The drip method begins with steps A and B as the floating method does. These steps balance the water temperature inside the bag. Once you have achieved this, you need to:

1. Empty the contents of the bag into the bucket. Remember to do this as carefully as possible so as not to stress or injure the creatures in them. It's also essential not to expose them to the air, so make sure they stay submerged as you empty the bag.

2. At this stage, the plastic tubing or pipes come into play. You need to run a drip line from your aquarium or tank to the bucket or buckets. It's important to control the flow so that the tube or pipe releases water very slowly. You could buy a control valve or make one by tying a fairly loose knot in the tube or pipe. It's also a good idea to fasten the pipe or tube to something so it stays securely in place.

3. It's not difficult to begin the siphoning process for the drip method. Suck on the end of the pipe or tube until water begins to flow through it from the tank or aquarium. You must then adjust the knot or valve so that the pipe releases only 2 to 4 drips per second.

4. When the amount or volume of water in the bucket has doubled you need to carefully and slowly discard half of it. Reinsert the tube and double the water volume again.

5. Transfer the fish etc. in the bucket(s) to the tank or aquarium. Again one must be very careful not to expose them to the air.

   If necessary, the more delicate organisms can be scooped out of the bucket in a specimen bag and then the bag should be submerged in the tank. Once the creatures are out of the bag, seal it underwater and remove it from the tank.

Be careful not to release too much of the diluted water into the aquarium. The water in the bag and bucket(s) must be discarded.

Some tips and rules with acclimation

- Don't rush the acclimation process; be patient.
- Some fish can appear to have died either before you begin acclimation or during the process. Don't assume they are dead. Continue with acclimation and quite often they will revive.
- Don't place an air-stone or introduce air through a pipe or tube into the shipping bag or bucket(s). Doing so increases the pH levels far too quickly and will expose your creatures to ammonia, which is lethal for them.
- Keep the aquarium lights off for at least 4 hours after you introduce new inhabitants into the tank or aquarium, as this will help them to adjust more easily to their new environment.

And a final thought…

There is a further stage that could or even should be introduced as part of introducing new stock into a tank or aquarium: the use of a quarantine tank. A quarantine tank, as the name implies, is a separate tank in which new arrivals are kept for two weeks or so before they are introduced into the main tank.

Doing this will greatly reduce the chances that newly arrived fish or invertebrates will introduce parasites or diseases that will infect your existing stock. It also gives the tank owner a chance to monitor the newcomers and make sure they are healthy, adjusting and eating well. It's not as easy to assess these factors once they are in with all the other creatures in the main tank.

Chapter 9: Caring for your Betta

1) Basic maintenance

It will be no surprise by now to hear that a tank is a fair amount of work. The fact that so many avid aquarists and hobbyists all over the world perform all the tasks that are necessary is proof of how wonderful having a healthy, colourful tank stocked with *Betta splendens* and other fascinating creatures is!

What can be very helpful is to draw up a schedule for regular and routine tank maintenance. In addition to feeding the inhabitants of the aquarium, the owner needs to carry out of number of tasks regularly. The basic ones are:

- Clean out the filter
- Clean out the container connected to the skimmer
- Check the various water parameters: temperature, pH, calcium, phosphate and nitrates
- Check to ensure that all the equipment is still working
- Replace 25% of the water in the tank
- Top up the tank
- Remove any dirt or detritus
- Monitor the condition of all the inhabitants of the tank.

These tasks are broken down by frequency in more detail later. As a rough guideline it is recommended by experienced aquarists that one checks:

- Equipment: daily
- Temperature: weekly
- Water change: once or twice a month.

Tip: Unplug the heater or heaters before you work on a tank! If you don't, and water levels change in such a way that they impact on the heater, you run the risk of cracking or breaking the glass in the tank or overheating or even burning out the heater.

2) Preparing water for your tank

One can't – or certainly experienced aquarists strongly advise against – just using tap water in an aquarium because it contains substances that are damaging to the water quality and therefore to the creatures living in the tank. Specifically, tap water usually contains chlorine and various heavy metals.

If one needs to top-up a tank, replace some of the water or mix up a solution, one must use treated tap water, bottled water or distilled water that has not passed through copper pipes during the distillation process.

Why you shouldn't use tap water in an aquarium

The water supplied in towns and cities is put through purification processes. However, this does not mean it is safe to use in a tank. If one does use it, one is likely to encounter problems.

Tap water often contains chlorine and the attendant chloramine bonds. One can use a de-chlorinating product but while they do remove chlorine, they don't usually break the chloramine bonds. You could look for a product, however, that specifically deals with chloramines.

In addition, tap water contains metals and, sometimes, bacteria. There are often heavy metals such as iron and copper in this water. These are often lethal for the fish and other creatures in a tank. The bacteria may be there because some strains will survive the chlorine used to treat the water. Once these bugs are in your aquarium, they will have a chance to flourish and infect your precious stock.

Furthermore, tap water – even in developed countries – does contain numerous elements and compounds that do belong in water such as silicates, phosphates and nitrates. The problem arises because these are toxic to fish and because tap water often contains high levels or high concentrations of these unwanted substances.

Treating tap water

Treating or pre-treating tap water is not always a great deal of work but some options can be more expensive than others. There are various routes one can take.

You could treat tap water with chlorine in order to kill any bacteria that may be in it. This is a simple option but it is not a very good one for two reasons.

1. You will remove most or even all the bacteria but the water will still contain heavy metals like iron and copper and minerals and trace elements such as nitrates and phosphate that will cause algae to flourish.

2. You will have to de-chlorinate the water before you can use it because chlorine is also not a friend to your fish and the other creatures in your tank or aquarium!

As with so much else, you can choose the way you will obtain the clean, good quality water necessary for your tank:

✓ Use *a basic water filter*. This is the most cost effective option but not necessarily the best one in terms of quality. You can obtain a freestanding filter of some kind or one that fits onto the tap. The latter is less cumbersome and time consuming to use

✓ A *carbon filtration system* is more effective than a regular water filter because these filters remove metals, phenols (acidic, organic compounds) and chlorine. A carbon filter is also said to reduce or even eliminate odours from the water.

  There are various types of carbon and carbon-based filters that are commercially available or one could make one.

✓ Perhaps the best type of water filter or filtration system is the *Reverse Osmosis (RO) or Deionization (DI) filtration unit*. The optimal system is thought to be one that is a RO DI combination.

These combined RO/DI systems are expensive but many aquarists believe they are worth the initial cost. The reason is that they save one a great deal by helping to preserve high water quality and so avoid many issues that are both difficult and costly to deal with. In effect, they are thought to pay for themselves.

- ✓ Instead of filtering water you could *buy fresh, filtered water* from local water companies. It is very important, though, to make sure that the producer and bottler uses a good, reliable filtration system, preferably a RO/DI system of some kind.
- ✓ *Buy bottles of distilled water* from commercial companies. The only word of caution here is to ensure that the distiller does not use copper pipes because if they do you may be introducing that undesirable metal into the tank water. You need to make enquiries about distillation processes before you use the water.

One factor to keep in mind when you are deciding on where and how you will get water is the size of the aquarium or tank. Naturally, the more water you need the more expensive some options will become. Others will be ruled out simply because they are not feasible or practical for you.

3) Topping up and cycling the water in a tank

A lower water level in a tank or aquarium is largely due to water evaporation. The tank should be kept at a constant level as this makes it much easier to regulate the various other levels and parameters.

Cycled water is also necessary for the health and well being of *Betta splendens.* It is water that contains colonies of 'good' bacteria that work to break down toxins in water and to convert them into substances that are far less harmful.

You can introduce cycled water by purchasing a biological conditioner from a reputable retailer and then adding the recommended amount to your tank. This should ideally be done before introducing fish or new fish into a tank.

4) Aquarium Salt

Salt is necessary in fresh water tanks and not only marine or salt water tanks. Clearly the levels of salinity will differ greatly. Aquarium Salt is easily available and one must just remember to follow the dosing and mixing instructions carefully. One also can't use ordinary table salt; this could be fatal for the residents of a tank.

The function of salt in a tank with your Bettas is twofold. Firstly, salt prevents fish from contracting a number of parasites and diseases. Secondly, Bettas breathe more easily in water than contains some salt.

5) Water changes

Water changes are one of the most important maintenance and care tasks any aquarium or tank owner has to perform. If water changes are neglected the overall water quality will suffer and all of the important water parameters will be out of the correct ranges. The effects of this could include algae blooms, murky water and – worst of all – sick or dead fish.

It is recommended that 25% of the water in the tank should be changed every week. A full or 100% water change is suggested every 2 or 3 months. By doing so one removes dirt and waste matter from the tank and replaces important elements that are necessary for tank health.

6) Standard tank maintenance schedules

Different tank owners will approach tank maintenance differently. The size of the tank and how many fish and other organisms live in it also affects how often certain tasks must be carried out.

While there may be some differing opinions in terms of when to do what, all aquarists agree that regular, routine maintenance is essential. It can be helpful to break tasks down as follows:

Daily maintenance checklist

- Check and adjust the water temperature
- Ensure all the equipment is running correctly
- Remove uneaten food and other matter that will decay
- Observe all the inhabitants for signs of ill health and stress
- Empty and rinse out the protein skimmer cup
- Check for leaks
- Ensure that all cords and tubes are still correctly connected and not leaking.

Weekly maintenance checklist

- Test levels of nitrate, ammonia, calcium, phosphate and nitrite and take corrective steps if necessary.
- Test pH levels.
- If you have a lot of creatures in your tank you must replace 10% of the water.
- Rinse out pre-filters, filters and the tube running to the protein skimmer.
- Remove any algae from the inside of the tank's sides by scraping it off or by using an algae magnet. These devices can be purchased from reputable retailers.

Bi-weekly to monthly maintenance checklist

The day before, or two days before, you do any major maintenance work on a tank you must check the pH levels, as they do tend to drop over time. If adjustments are necessary, they should be made before you carry out any cleaning, as it will help to guard against pH shock.

Bi-weekly and monthly tasks are:

- Change 10% of the water in the tank or aquarium. A partial water change should in fact be done weekly if you have a lot of creatures in the tank.
- Remove algae, deposits and build-up on tank surfaces.
- Remove chemical deposits from the light fixtures. A small quantity of white vinegar on a clean sponge is effective against calcium.
- Carefully and gently vacuum the substrate to remove any debris.
- Check all equipment such as power sources for damage.
- Check the filters and replace disposable filters that have become dirty, clogged or saturated.
- Clear out the protein skimmer hose and valve. These valves and tubes can also be soaked in vinegar water to remove any calcium. However, they must be very thoroughly rinsed in fresh water afterwards.

Bi-monthly maintenance checklist

As with bi-weekly and monthly maintenance one must test and correct pH levels a day or two before working on the aquarium.

- Clean out all tubes, hoses and pipes. Over time they become clogged by a build-up of compounds and detritus in the tank. An aquarium brush can be used to achieve this. Various sizes and thicknesses of brushes are available commercially.
- Avid and experienced aquarists also clean out important items of equipment such as heaters and powerheads.

- If your tank system uses activated charcoal for filtration the carbon must be replaced. If it is left for too long the carbon becomes so saturated that it begins to release toxins and impurities back into the water.
- Perform a 100% water change.

Bi-annual and annual maintenance checklist

- Replace light bulbs or lighting tubes because over time the colour and intensity of the light they provide changes either due to aging or damage from calcium build-up.

7) Being prepared for power failures or outages

A loss of power is a fact of life for most people. Weather and the state of power grids can impact on the reliability of power supply. Not having power can constitute anything from an inconvenience to being life threatening.

For the creatures in your tank or aquarium, the loss of power is always life threatening. One vital system for aquarium residents is temperature control. Filtration becomes a problem later on but it too will become crucial. Light is more important for certain creatures than it is for others including fish. Tank owners must therefore be prepared for a loss of power.

The first option is *battery operated systems*. There is a range of commercially available equipment that runs on batteries. These can provide oxygen, heat and filtration, all of which the fish and other occupants in a tank require in order to survive. These systems are usually the least costly and the easiest to put in place.

The second possibility is an *Uninterrupted Power Supply* (UPS). These units are traditionally used to keep personal computers going for a while following a loss of power. However, one can also connect essential tank equipment to one. The benefits of a UPS are firstly that it will come on automatically and, secondly, more powerful units can run for longer than battery operated equipment. The fact that the unit will come on automatically means that your tank's creatures will have emergency help even if you are not at home when the power goes out.

Finally, tank owners could invest in a *power generator*. Given they are not cheap to buy they should be viewed as an investment that will prevent costly livestock losses. As an added advantage, if a larger and more powerful generator were purchased, it would have the capacity to meet household power needs in addition to keeping all the aquarium systems running.

Generators are sold in several sizes or capacities and can run on diesel, petrol or even propane. Retailers and suppliers will be able to offer information and advice in terms of the best model and type for your specific requirements.

Regardless of which source of alternative and emergency power you select, it will make a great difference in terms of ensuring your tank's inhabitants stay fit and healthy and reducing your stress levels in the event of a loss of power.

8) A summary of tank conditions

There's a great deal to remember in terms of the parameters for various water and other environmental factors in an aquarium. If various levels and conditions are not correct, a tank owner will be faced with high mortality rates amongst aquarium inhabitants, extra costs and a great deal of extra work.

A summary of the primary levels and parameters for the type of reef tank used for Betta fish are as follows:

- Temperature: 75 – 80° Fahrenheit or 24 – 27° Celsius
- pH: 6.5 – 8
- Calcium: Less than 0.2 parts per million (ppm)
- Nitrate: Less than 1.0 parts per million (ppm)
- Phosphate: Less than 0.2 parts per million (ppm)
- Nitrite and ammonia: Should not be detectable

Chapter 10: Feeding your Betta

1) What to feed your Betta

The *Betta splendens'* mouth is upturned, which allows it to feed at the surface. Its natural diet is water-bound creatures including mosquito larvae, small crustaceans and zooplankton and small insects.

In the wild, Bettas are opportunistic feeders and not predators. In other words, it will eat whatever food it comes across rather than hunting for it. These fish are not omnivorous and therefore only eat plant matter if they are forced to be due to lack of food.

You can feed Bettas brine shrimp, daphnia and dried bloodworms or tubifex worms. Commercial freeze dried or pellet foods that are specially formulated for *Betta splendens* will contain all of these food sources in addition to providing the various minerals and vitamins these fish need in order to stay healthy and to retain their glorious colours.

Bettas should not be fed fatty foods. In fact, they are unlikely to eat them and the uneaten food will foul the water. If the fish do eat these foods they may cause problems or sluggishness at the least.

2) How often to feed Betta fish

Different tank owners have different feeding schedules. However, feeding guidelines seem to be:

- Feed your fish once or twice a day
- Feed at set or regular times if possible
- Don't feed them on one day a week in order to 'rest' their digestive systems.

The golden rule is, "Do Not Overfeed". Overfeeding pollutes the tank and can even kill fish.

3) How much food to give your Betta fish

There are guidelines one can use in order to determine how much food to give your *Betta splendens*. If you feed them once a day, give them what they will eat in about 2 minutes.

If you give them food two times a day it should not be more than they can eat in approximately 3 minutes.

4) Dealing with excess food or leftovers

Uneaten food that remains in the tank and floats around in the water and / or gets stuck in cracks and crevices pose a health risk in the tank. This type of debris is dangerous because it can lead to algae blooms, bacterial outbreaks and reduction in overall water quality.

A detritus pack or clean-up crew in the form of catfish and snails help a great deal with this issue.

Chapter 11: Health management

There are several factors that affect the health of *Betta splendens* and other fish species:

- *Water quality* is considered by many aquarists to be the most important factor of all when it comes to ensuring that fish stay healthy. This includes temperature and the absence of toxins in addition to general cleanliness.
- The second crucial factor in maintaining health is *diet*. This encompasses both what one feeds to fish and how often and how much.

Knowing this means that one can already go a long way to keeping Bettas healthy.

Setting up a tank for your *Betta splendens* is both a time consuming and a costly business. Once it has been done and you are carrying out routine maintenance, the last thing you want is an outbreak of disease in your aquarium.

Apart from selecting stock with care and monitoring your tank inhabitant's health, there is another step you can take: make use of a quarantine tank.

1) A quarantine tank

What is a quarantine tank for?

Most aquarists or tank owners don't have a quarantine tank because of the expense of setting one up and the maintenance. However, quarantine tanks don't need to be big or costly. Furthermore, the benefits these tanks provide mean that they in effect pay for themselves.

Quarantine tanks, as the name implies, keep new or sick fish or other creatures away from the others in order to prevent the spread of infections, parasites or other medical problems.

However, these tanks have a second, very important, function and that is that they make it easier to treat or medicate sick fish. This second function of these tanks gives rise to their alternative names of treatment or hospital tanks.

When you are dealing with an infected fish you need to do two things. Firstly, the infected fish or fishes must be kept away from the healthy ones. Secondly, you need to be able to medicate the sick fish without exposing healthy fish to medications that could harm them or cause them to build a resistance to the medication. Some fish medications can be particularly harmful to some molluscs, amphibians and invertebrates.

By using a quarantine tank, you can achieve both of these objectives and deal with the medical problem faster and without knock-on effects in the tank and on the tank's general population.

When a quarantine tank should be used

These important tanks are used on two different occasions.

The fist time a quarantine tank is important or useful is when you buy new stock for your tank. A quarantine tank allows you to isolate newcomers before you introduce them into the main aquarium. This gives you the opportunity to make sure that they are healthy.

The second situation you would benefit greatly from using a tank of this kind is when you discover that a new fish or one in the main tank is sick and therefore in need of isolation and treatment.

Further benefits of quarantine tanks

There is a range of additional benefits associated with these tanks. Firstly, because quarantine tanks are usually fairly small (often about 10 gallons or 45.5 UK litres or 38 US litres or slightly more), one uses less medication and can monitor and control dosing far more easily. This also greatly reduces the risk of accidental overdosing. All these factors make treatment more effective and save you some money.

In addition, it is much easier to watch and examine a sick fish or other creature in a smaller and less populated tank. One can assess physical factors such as colour, eyes, the condition of fins and scales, growths and so forth.

With both sick and newly arrived creatures a quarantine tank offers an ideal opportunity to make sure they are eating well and even what foods they respond to better. Again, this is much harder or even impossible to do in a large or main tank.

Finally, a quarantine tank acts as a halfway house for newcomers, where they can start to settle and recover from the stress of transport or shipping before moving into the main tank. This often makes acclimation to the main tank easier.

Setting up a quarantine tank

The equipment required for a quarantine tank is essentially a much reduced or streamlined version of what is needed for the large or main tank. In addition to the tank itself, one needs to buy substrate, a filter, a thermometer, an air pump, a heater and suitable lighting. It should be noted, though, that some aquarists don't even use a substrate in these tanks.

One also must have a dedicated water test kit and aquarium nets for use in the quarantine tank as one can't use any equipment from it in the main tank or vice versa as this creates the risk of contaminating the main tank and its inhabitants.

It's a good idea to have a quarantine tank that is bare or without décor because porous materials such as rocks, sand and gravel can absorb medications. This means that your fish are not receiving the correct dose.

However, because some fish like *Betta splendens*, and other species that are shy, like or need to have hiding places you will need to supply some. However, they should be made of non-porous materials or items such as sections of plastic pipe, for example.

Placing sick fish into a quarantine tank

As with introducing new and healthy fish into a tank, one ideally should go through an acclimation or transition phase with sick fish going from the main tank into a quarantine or treatment tank.

You need to remove the sick fish and, if possible, use one of the acclimation methods. If the fish is too sick, then one has no choice but to place it straight into the other tank with its different, but clean, water conditions. For this reason, the quarantine tank should mimic the water conditions and parameters in the main tank as closely as possible.

Finally, remember to wash your hands with antibacterial soap after handling a sick fish and the net you moved it in. This will ensure that you don't inadvertently infect other fish when you work on or in the main tank.

Quarantine tank maintenance

Ideally one should have one quarantine tank for fish and another for non-fish. It's also extremely important that the quarantine tank and equipment is disinfected between uses. A mild (2-5%) chlorine bleach solution is an effective disinfectant for this purpose. However, one must ensure that all of the chlorine is removed before using the tank again.

The quarantine tank and all the associated equipment must also be thoroughly dried because drying kills many aquatic pathogens, but unfortunately not all of them.

2) Common illnesses and health problems

Common signs of illness in Betta and other fish

While one can acquire the knowledge to make a much more accurate diagnosis in terms of the health issue a fish is suffering from, there are some general signs and symptoms all tank owners should be on the look-out for:

- Loss of, or marked reduction in, appetite

- Growths or lumps
- Loss of colour
- Scales are rough or sticking out
- Listlessness
- Unusual or erratic movements
- Tattered fins or tail
- Swollen belly or very thin body
- White spots or fungus on the body
- White or red patches in the mouth
- Red or swollen gills
- Laboured or unusual breathing.

If you run the usual water quality and parameter tests and they are all as they should be, then you need to establish what specifically the fish is suffering from. Without an accurate diagnosis it is hard, if not impossible, to successfully treat a sick creature. If you don't feel up to the task, a vet or specialist should be consulted.

Please note that the treatments suggested in this chapter are not guaranteed to work; factors such as correct diagnosis, the severity of the particular illness and how advanced it is all impact on outcome.

Preventing common health problems

There are steps that one can and should take that go a very long way to guarding against the common health issues that fish including *Betta splendens* are susceptible to:

- ✓ Use a quarantine tank to screen new fish and isolate and treat sick fish
- ✓ Maintain good water quality through testing, dosing when needed, regular partial water changes, maintaining the correct pH and temperature
- ✓ Ensure effective filtration, correct water temperature and lighting levels and adequate oxygenation

- ✓ Don't put too many fish in a tank, as overcrowding causes stress-related problems and cross infection
- ✓ Perform all the necessary maintenance on the tank to ensure optimal conditions at all times
- ✓ Use appropriate foods and feeding routines.

Fish diseases and ailments

A) Cryptocaryon irritans

Cryptocaryon is more commonly known as White Spot Disease or Ichthyophthirius (Ich). It is caused by a protozoan (a single celled organism) called *Cryptocaryon irritans,* which infests fish by burrowing into their skin and later the gills and forming cysts.

It is not a rapidly progressing illness and if it is detected early it can be very successfully treated. However, if it is neglected the consequences are very serious and can destroy an entire fish population and infest the entire tank.

The life cycle of Cryptocaryon irritans

The life cycle of this protozoan is significant both in terms of the effect on the infected fish and why it poses such a huge risk to all the fish in a tank.

The earliest stage of the life of *Cryptocaryon irritans* is when the immature cells, called tomites, are released when the cyst in the host bursts. These tomites float in the water until they find a new host and attach themselves to it.

The next stage in the life cycle is that of a parasitic trophont. These nasty organisms burrow into the flesh or gills of the host fish and begin to feed on the tissue at that site.

Once the trophont has consumed enough, it forms a cyst. These are called inactive tomonts. The cysts may be stuck in the surface mucous of the fish or buried deep in their tissue.

Within 6 to 10 days the cells inside the cysts reproduce. Each one becomes a tomite. When the cyst is mature it ruptures and releases hundreds of tomites into the water. Each one will search for a host.

In other words, the cycle repeats itself and the only difference is that each time there are more tomites. It is easy to see how easily an entire tank can become infected.

Symptoms

The first sign of White Spot Disease or Ich are very small white spots on the fins and body of the fish that is host to *Cryptocaryon irritans*. These spots can be as small as grains of salt, which is why a tank owner must be vigilant, and observe and monitor fish regularly. This protozoan only moves from the skin to the gills when it has reached the parasitic trophont stage.

Infected fish will also rub themselves against objects in the tank. This is an effort to dislodge the parasites on their skin. When the parasites have attacked the fish's gills, the symptoms become far more marked and severe. The gills become blocked by mucous, tissue debris and the tomonts themselves. This results in laboured breathing.

At this advanced stage the fish will have stopped eating, will be very listless and have lost colour in the places where the trophonts destroyed pigment cells in the skin.

There will also be lesions or wounds in the skin, which then become infected by other bacteria.

Treatment of Ich

Treatment needs to be effective for each stage of the life cycle of the *Cryptocaryon irritans*. Not all treatment options work on more than one stage. For example, copper effectively combats the free-swimming tomites but does nothing to deal with trophonts that have burrowed into tissue. To deal with this advanced stage of the infestation one needs to use a combination of formalin and freshwater treatments. These are administered over an extended period through baths and dips.

A quarantine tank is essential to deal with this problem. You need to generate vigorous aeration in the tank as part of the treatment. Two containers of different types of treatment water also need to be prepared.

In the first one the water should include a formalin product. It is vital that one follows the directions on the packaging so that the solution is correctly mixed. This is the treatment water. It should also contain another product in addition to the formalin that will counteract the ammonia that is a harmful and inevitable by-product of this treatment process. High levels will cause a condition known as ammonia burn.

If you don't have a formalin treatment product, emergency treatment can be provided in the form of a freshwater bath. It won't cure the infestation but it can give a sick fish some relief by flushing some mucous out of the gills and removing some parasites from the skin. This eases breathing and reduces irritation. Place the fish in the hyposalinity dip and then back in the quarantine tank. A suitable formalin solution should be obtained as soon as possible.

The second container should contain water with lowered salinity. Hyposalinity or the lowering of specific gravity to approximately 1.010 ppm won't treat or cure the infestation but it does help to prevent re-infestation. It is also used as a dip for fish that have been in the treatment water. This low salinity water helps to remove dead or weak parasites or mucous from the affected fish.

The treatment process must be handled carefully and accurately as fish requiring these steps are already very sick – perhaps even dying – and weak.

The first stage is to gently place the infested fish into the container containing the formalin treatment product. The sicker the fish is, the more careful one must be. A seriously infested fish may not be able to tolerate the treatment bath for more than a few minutes if at all or may even die during the treatment.

When dealing with such badly affected fish another option is to dilute the solution further, which may make a longer dip time possible. Less badly affected fish can remain in the treatment bath longer (anything up to an hour).

The stage after the treatment bath is a dip in the second container that contains low salinity water. A very stressed or shocked fish may only cope with a 30 second dip. Less severely affected fish can tolerate 1 minute or even 2 minutes. Once this dip is finished, the fish should be returned to the quarantine tank.

Fish affected by *Cryptocaryon irritans* should be kept in the quarantine tank for the duration of the life cycle of the protozoan / a minimum of 4 weeks. The treatment will continue as directed by the formalin product manufacturers. It is also recommended that an antibacterial be added to the treatment regimen so that one also deals with secondary bacterial infections.

During the period that you are treating your fish there should be no fish in the main tank. This will ensure that all the protozoa, at each cycle of their life, in the tank die off as they are unable to find fish hosts.

Words of caution

- Don't leave fish unattended in the treatment bath or the dip. You need to watch them closely and constantly and remove them immediately if they show signs of distress or stress.
- Formaldehyde is a toxic substance and should be used with caution and due care. It should only be used as directed, for parasite infestations and fungal diseases in fish. It is highly toxic to invertebrates and can be harmful to fish if they are exposed to it too often.
- Ensure that the treatment product you select is effective against *Cryptocaryon* specifically as some are for other types of Ich but are not effective against this protozoan.

Preventing re-infestation

If you don't eliminate the *Cryptocaryon irritans* from the main tank your fish will be re-infested regardless of how effectively you treated the fish themselves. As previously mentioned, the main tank must not house any fish for at least 4 weeks.

Creating hyposalinity in the tank speeds up the *Cryptocaryon's* life cycle, which helps while you dose the tank water. However, one can only use this technique if your tank is a fish only tank or not a reef tank. Hyposalinity is not an option if you have corals and various types of invertebrates. There are various solutions available for reef tanks that can be added to the water to destroy *Cryptocaryon* at each stage of the life cycle.

Before you can reintroduce your fish back into the main tank, you must change filtering materials, clean filters very thoroughly and do a full water change. Then run a full battery of tests to ensure that all the water and environmental parameters are correct.

B) Brooklynella

Brooklynella is more commonly known as Betta fish Disease. Despite this common name, it is not only Betta fish that become infested. This disease is another form of Ich and is caused by a protozoan (a single celled organism) called *Brooklynella hostilis,* which infests fish by burrowing into their skin and later the gills and forming cysts.

Brooklynella, unlike *Cryptocaryon,* is a very rapidly progressing illness and can kill a fish within a few hours or days. This means that immediate diagnosis and treatment are essential to prevent the loss of all the fish in the tank.

Symptoms

The signs and symptoms of this aggressive disease are dramatic and distressing to see. *Brooklynella,* again unlike *Cryptocaryon,* attacks the gills first. In its efforts to dislodge the parasite, a fish will scrape against rocks, corals or other hard surfaces.

As the gills become increasingly affected, fish begin to breathe rapidly and will gasp for air at the surface of the water. It will usually remain near the surface or where there is a strong stream of water entering the tank. This inability to breathe is due to a build-up of thick mucous that clogs the gills. Hardly surprisingly, fish with *Brooklynella* stop eating, their colour fades and they become very lethargic.

The most distinctive symptom of this very serious fish disease begins as the disease progresses: the heavy production of slime or mucous which covers the fish's body. This thick, white coating begins at the head and then spreads to the rest of the body. This is often accompanied by lesions on the skin. These lesions often become infected by bacteria and need separate treatment.

Treatment

Treatment recommendations include a solution of malachite green or copper sulphate used in conjunction with formaldehyde. However, many aquarists believe the most effective treatment for *Brooklynella* is formaldehyde used on its own along with a hyposalinity dip. Treatment should be administered over an extended period.

A quarantine tank is essential to deal with this problem. You need to generate vigorous aeration in the tank as part of the treatment. Two containers of different types of treatment water also need to be prepared.

In the first one the water should include a formalin product. It is vital that one follows the directions on the packaging so that the solution is correctly mixed. This is the treatment water. It should also contain another product in addition to the formalin that will counteract the ammonia that is a harmful and inevitable by-product of this treatment process. High levels will cause a condition known as ammonia burn.

If you don't have a formalin treatment product, emergency treatment can be provided in the form of a freshwater bath. It won't cure the infestation but it can give a sick fish some relief by flushing some mucous out of the gills and removing some parasites from the skin. This eases breathing and reduces irritation. Place the fish in the hyposalinity dip and then back in the quarantine tank. A suitable formalin solution should be obtained as soon as possible.

The second container should contain water with lowered salinity. Hyposalinity or the lowering of specific gravity to approximately 1.010 ppm won't treat or cure the infestation but it does help to prevent re-infestation. It is also used as a dip for fish that have been in the treatment water. This low salinity water helps to remove dead or weak parasites and some mucous from the affected fish.

The treatment process must be handled carefully and accurately as fish requiring these steps are already very sick – perhaps even dying – and weak.

The first stage is to gently place the infested fish or fishes into the container containing the formalin treatment product. The sicker the fish is, the more careful one must be. A seriously infested fish may not be able to tolerate the treatment bath for more than a few minutes if at all or may even die during the treatment.

When dealing with such sick and weak fish another option is to dilute the solution further which may make a longer dip time possible. Less badly affected fish can remain in the treatment bath longer (anything up to an hour).

The stage after the treatment bath is a dip in the second container that contains low salinity water. A very stressed or shocked fish may only cope with a 30 second dip. Less severely affected fish can tolerate 1 minute or even 2 minutes. Once this dip is finished the fish should be returned to the quarantine tank.

Fish affected by *Brooklynella* should be kept in the quarantine tank for the duration of the life cycle of the protozoan or at least 4 weeks. The treatment will continue as directed by the formalin product manufacturers. It is also strongly recommended that an antibacterial be added to the treatment regimen so that one also deals with secondary bacterial infections.

During the period that you are treating your fish there should be no fish in the main tank. This will ensure that all the protozoa, at each cycle of their life, in the tank die off as they are unable to find fish hosts.

Ensure that the treatment product you select is effective against *Brooklynella* specifically as some are for other types of Ich but are not effective against this protozoan.

C) Oodinium

Oodinium, also known as Velvet Disease or Coral Fish Disease, is caused by a dinoflagellate (a protist or parasitic, single-celled microorganism) called *Amyloodinium ocellatum.* This nasty type of infestation is another of the Ich diseases.

Amyloodinium, like *Brooklynella,* is a very rapidly progressing illness and can kill a fish within a few hours or days. This organism also reproduces very fast. This means that immediate diagnosis and treatment is essential to prevent the loss of all the fish in the tank.

Symptoms

The symptoms of *Amyloodinium* are very similar to those of *Brooklynella* infestation and this organism also attacks the fish's gills first.

An infected fish will scrape against rocks, corals or other hard surfaces in an effort to dislodge the parasites. As the gills become increasingly affected, fish begin to breathe rapidly and will gasp for air at the surface of the water. One often notices breathing difficulties when fish stay at the surface or where there is a flow of water. This inability to breathe is due to a build-up of mucous that clogs the gills. The fish will stop eating, their colour fades and they become very lethargic.

Unlike with *Cryptocaryon, Amyloodinium* starts in the gills and then spreads to the body. Tiny cysts on the fish's body and fins become visible. They look like grains of salt and resemble the first sign of White Spot Disease / Ich or *Cryptocaryon.*

What is different, however, is that these cysts at this advanced stage of the disease give the fish a tan or golden colouring and a velvet-like film coats the whole fish that is what gives rise to the name Velvet Disease. The fish's eyes will also cloud over in the final stage of the disease.

The life cycle of Amyloodinium or Oodinium

Like *Cryptocaryon, Amyloodinium ocellatum* has 3 stages in its life-cycle.

The first stage in the life cycle is when free-swimming cells, called dinospores, are released when a mature cyst in the host bursts. These dinospores float in the water until they find a new host and they can survive for up to 8 days without a host. Some strains can survive for a month in cooler water.

In the next stage of the life cycle, the dinospores loose their ability to swim. They become parasitic trophozoites, which attach to their host by means of a feeding filament. They attack the gill tissue of the fish and begin to feed on it. The trophozoite will feed off its host for 3 to 7 days, at which point they are mature. They may drop off the host, remain in the mucous membrane covering the host or stay buried in the host's flesh. The trophozoites remaining in the fish then form cysts.

At the encysted stage, the organism is called a tomont. Within 5 days the cells inside the cysts reproduce. When the cyst is mature it ruptures and releases hundreds of tomites or dinospores into the water. Each one will search for a host.

The life cycle then repeats and the only difference is that each time there are more free-swimming dinospores. An entire tank can become infected very quickly.

Treatment

Treatment needs to be effective for each stage of the life cycle of the *Amyloodinium*. Not all treatment options work on more than one stage. To deal with the advanced stage of the infestation one needs to use a combination of treatments. These are administered over an extended period through baths and dips.

A quarantine tank is essential to deal with this problem. Two containers of different types of treatment water also need to be prepared. *Amyloodinium* can survive a broad salinity range (anything from 3 to 45 ppm). As a result, a hyposalinity dip or bath is not at all effective against this parasite.

In the first container the water should include a formalin or formalin and copper solution product. It is vital that one follows the directions on the packaging so that the solution is correctly mixed. This is the treatment water. It should also contain another product in addition to the formalin that will counteract the ammonia that is a harmful and inevitable by-product of this treatment process.

If you don't have a treatment product, emergency treatment can be provided in the form of a freshwater bath until you can find a treatment solution.

The second container should contain a freshwater dip. This water should have a slightly reduced pH and a specific gravity of 1.001. Some aquarists also add the compound known as Methylene Blue.

The first stage is to place the infected fish into the treatment water. When dealing with such badly affected fish another option is to dilute the solution further which may make a longer dip time possible.

The stage after the treatment bath is a dip in the second container that holds the fresh water solution as described above. An effective duration for the dip is between 3 and 5 minutes. Don't worry if a fish appears dead and even 'lies down'. This behaviour is a normal initial reaction to being in the fresh water solution. After a minute or two the fish should perk up significantly.

There are two reasons why a freshwater solution is so effective against this parasite. The first is that with *Amyloodinium* the cysts are not as deeply embedded as they are in cases of *Cryptocaryon.*

Secondly, the membrane of the cells of the Oodinium cyst isn't strong enough to withstand the change in osmotic pressure caused by a move to fresh water.

As a result of this pressure the cysts burst. However, in order to achieve this, the fish must remain in the dip for 3 minutes. Once this dip is finished the fish should be returned to the quarantine tank.

Fish affected by *Amyloodinium* should be kept in the quarantine tank for the duration of the life cycle of the parasite. The treatment will continue as directed by the treatment product manufacturers. It is also recommended that an antibacterial be added to the treatment regimen so that one also deals with secondary bacterial infections.

During the period that you are treating your fish there should be no fish in the main tank. This will ensure that all the dinospores and cysts in the tank die.

Preventing re-infection

If you don't eliminate *Amyloodinium* from the main tank your fish will be re-infested regardless of how effectively you treated the fish themselves. As previously mentioned the main tank must not house any fish for at least 4 weeks.

Raising the tank temperature to 85 or even 90° Fahrenheit or 29.5 to 32° Celsius will speed up the life cycle. There are also various solutions available for reef tanks that can be added to the water to destroy *Amyloodinium* dinospores.

Before you can reintroduce your fish back into the main tank you must change filtering materials, clean filters very thoroughly and do a full water change. Then run a full battery of tests to ensure that all the water and environmental parameters are correct.

Ensure that the treatment product you select is effective against *Amyloodinium* specifically as some are for other types of Ich but are not effective against this parasite.

D) Tail Rot and Fin Rot

Tail and Fin Rot are thought to be caused by injuries such as nipping by other fish, poor tank conditions or a bacterial infection following injury. They can also be a secondary condition caused by Fish Tuberculosis.

Symptoms

The signs and symptoms of Fin or Tail Rot are easy to spot. The tail and / or fin look frayed and show signs of disintegration. In very severe cases the tail and fins can be reduced to stumps because the tissue has broken down entirely.

Other signs are bleeding along the edges of the fins or tail, red or inflamed-looking areas at the base of the tail or fin, exposed fin rays (the soft, flexible 'rods' that run the length of the fin) and ulcers on the skin. In fish with advanced Rot, their eyes also become cloudy.

Treatment

Given there are several possible causes of Tail and Fin Rot, the first steps must be to establish the cause and place the affected fish in a quarantine tank. Once the cause has been determined, one must remedy it if possible and treat the fish or the water. For example, if the damage is due to attacks by another fish, you will have to take steps to keep them apart, or if water quality is poor, that must be remedied immediately.

Regardless of the cause, you will probably have to use an antibiotic treatment; even if the rot is not bacterial in origin the damaged tissue will almost certainly be infected. The choice one has at this point is to either dose the fish or the water.

If an antibiotic is added to the water is it very important that the instructions are carefully followed with regards to dosage. In addition, be very cautious about adding medications to a main tank as they may adversely affect invertebrates and corals.

If the antibiotic is to be administered to the fish, one can mix it carefully in to flake food. Some aquarists suggest that one keeps fish a little hungry so that when the flakes mixed with antibiotic arrive they are eaten fast and the antibiotic isn't lost in the water.

Your local specialist or vet will be able to offer advice as to which antibiotic would be most suitable and to suggest an appropriate dose. Chloromycetin and Tetracyclines are often used in very small quantities.

Advanced Tail Rot and Fin Rot

Symptoms

The symptoms are similar to tail and fin rot except, as the name implies, they are far more advanced.

With this condition the fins and tail are eaten away entirely and reduced to stumps. The illness also progresses far quicker at this stage of the disease. When the tail and fins are gone, the bacteria that are usually involved begin to attack the body.

Even at this advanced stage the fish may survive for some weeks if it is being treated. Its ability to swim is lost entirely without fins and a tail. This condition cannot be reversed.

Treatment

This is also similar to the treatment for the earlier stages of the disease. However, a specialist may recommend that you use both an increased dose and several medications in combination.

E) Black Spot Disease

Black Spot Disease is caused by small parasitic worms. It gets its name from the black spots formed by the parasites. These marks are not nearly as numerous as the white ones characteristic of White Spot Disease or Ich. It is also not nearly as serious, although parasites are never desirable!

Symptoms

Other than the black spots on the fish's body, which are the primary sign, the other symptom is that the fish will move erratically and try to remove the irritating parasites by rubbing against hard surfaces such as rocks.

Treatment

If a fish is not badly infested, a 5 minute bath in freshwater should be enough to deal with these parasites. As with any treatment bath, the fish should be watched closely and removed as soon as it shows signs of becoming highly stressed.

For fish suffering from a more severe infestation, treatment with a solution of trichlorofon or copper is necessary. A copper- or trichlorofon-based solution can't be added to the main tank, as it will adversely affect invertebrates. The fish that require treatment must therefore be placed in a quarantine tank first.

Prevention

Placing new fish in a freshwater dip and then keeping them in a quarantine tank for a few weeks before introducing them to the main tank is one of the primary ways to ensure that this parasite is not introduced into your tank.

In addition, ensuring that the water quality is good at all times and that the other environmental parameters in the tank are always as they should be will prevent stress in the tank inhabitants. Stress affects fish badly as it damages their mucous coating. Weaknesses in this coating make the fish vulnerable, as parasites can gain hold far more easily. Finally, the use of a correctly installed ultraviolet (UV) sterilizer will also help to prevent outbreaks of this parasite.

F) Gill and Fin Flukes

These flukes are small, worm-like parasites that multiply very quickly. This is a highly infectious disease that is fatal if affected fish are not treated very quickly. What makes this parasite so dangerous is that they can clog the gills of the fish, which causes them to suffocate slowly.

Symptoms

As with other parasitic infestations, the affected fish will swim erratically and rub against hard surfaces as they try to dislodge the parasites. Fish with these flukes also exhibit rapid and laboured breathing and often have white patches on their bodies and cloudy eyes.

In severe cases, the worm-like parasites may sometimes be visible as thin, thread-like objects.

Treatment

A freshwater bath usually kills the majority of the parasites and brings the fish immediate relief from many of the symptoms. For fish that are more severely affected, a longer treatment bath of salt water and methylene blue may be required.

Prevention

Placing new fish in a freshwater dip and then keeping them in a quarantine tank for a few weeks before introducing them to the main tank is one of the primary ways to ensure that this parasite is not introduced into your tank.

In addition, ensuring that the water quality is good at all times and that the other environmental parameters in the tank are always as they should be will prevent stress in the tank inhabitants. Stress affects fish badly as it damages their mucous coating. Weaknesses in this coating make the fish vulnerable as parasites can gain hold far more easily.

Finally, the use of a correctly installed ultraviolet (UV) sterilizer will also help to prevent outbreaks of this parasite.

G) Lymphocystis

Lymphocystis is a fish disease that is caused by a virus. It is also known as Cauliflower Disease because of the appearance of the growths.

While fish that have this problem look really ill, the condition is rarely fatal. In addition, it may even clear up on its own if the water quality is very good.

Symptoms

The only symptom is the clumps of wart-like growths (that look like cauliflowers) that grow on the body of fish with this virus.

Treatment

Like with most viruses, there is no treatment for Lymphocystis. One can give fish a short freshwater dip but essentially the condition will go with time *if* water quality is optimal.

The danger with viral conditions is the possibility of secondary bacterial infections. If this occurs the fish should be placed in a quarantine tank and dosed with antibiotics.

Prevention

Placing new fish in a freshwater dip and then keeping them in a quarantine tank for a few weeks before introducing them to the main tank is one of the primary ways to ensure that this virus is not introduced into your tank.

Ensuring that high water quality is maintained in the tank at all times is the best deterrent for this condition.

In addition, ensuring that the water quality is good at all times and that the other environmental parameters in the tank are always as they should be will prevent stress in the tank inhabitants. Stress affects fish badly and makes them more likely to contract a viral infection.

H) Fungus

This disease, also called Ichthyophonus or CNS Disease, is usually associated with stress. It is also sometimes caused by poor water quality. This is not a very common disease and treatment is very difficult. The fungus is usually introduced into the tank when new creatures are introduced into it.

Symptoms

Fish suffering from this fungus develop skin that looks like sandpaper. They also darken in colour, become listless and have poor appetites.

Treatment

Treating this condition is not easy. Affected fish must be placed in a quarantine tank and dosed with a suitable anti-fungal medication. Your local retailer or vet will be able to recommend suitable products.

One must also ensure that water quality is good and that the fish is as stress-free as possible, as stress breaks down the immune system further, which in turn weakens the fish further and allows the condition to gain a stronger hold.

Prevention

Ensuring that high water quality is maintained and that all the environmental factors are optimal at all times is the best deterrent for this condition.

Correct water quality and environmental parameters will prevent stress in the tank inhabitants. Stress affects fish badly as it breaks down the mucous coating on the fish's skin and thereby makes them more vulnerable and likely to develop fungal problems.

Placing new fish in a freshwater dip and then keeping them in a quarantine tank for a few weeks before introducing them to the main tank is one of the primary ways to ensure that this virus is not introduced into your tank.

I) Mycobacterium marinum or Fish Tuberculosis

Mycobacterium marinum is also known as Fish Tuberculosis (TB). It is a very serious and invariably fatal bacterial infection. Not only does it pose a huge risk to fish, but also fish tank owners or aquarists can contract it too and suffer some serious health problems as a result.

These aggressive bacteria can survive in salt and fresh water, in soil and without a host for extended periods of time.

Symptoms

Fish that have contracted *Mycobacterium marinum* are affected in several dramatic ways. They loose colour and scales. They suffer from wasting and therefore become very thin.

In addition, they develop lesions on the skin and may develop skeletal deformities, the most obvious one being curvature of the spine.

Treatment

This serious illness is almost impossible to cure. Many aquarists believe it is kinder to euthanize a fish rather than let it suffer the ravages of the disease and the stress of treatments that are unlikely to help. The best way to prevent it spreading is drastic: euthanizing all the fish in the tank!

Apart from a desire to spare the fish suffering, aquarists are also reluctant to treat these fish as it exposes them to the bacteria and possible infection.

The medication that is usually used to treat this infection is Kanamycin / Kantrex. As with other forms of TB, treatment involves a combination of medications (at least 2), which are administered over an extended period - usually a minimum of three months.

The usual 'fixes' such as raising the water temperature, changing the water or raising salinity levels don't have any effect at all on *Mycobacterium marinum*, which thrives in warm water.

Prevention

The difficulty with treatment and the resulting high mortality rates make prevention very important with this disease. The first step in prevention is to keep fish happy / stress-free and well fed, as this will promote strong immunity. They will be more likely to be able to resist infection, at least initially.

Weak or injured fish are extremely vulnerable and should be moved into treatment or quarantine tanks as soon as possible if they show signs of the illness.

New fish must be placed in quarantine for several weeks before they are introduced into the main tank. All of the décor and the equipment that goes into the tanks must be sterilised.

If an entire aquarium and fish population has been affected by this highly infectious disease, it is essential that the tank be emptied and cleaned very thoroughly with bleach, rinsed with great care and then left to dry. It should not be restocked until the tank has been cleaned and is dry.

J) Popeye

Popeye is a condition rather than a disease. It is also known as Exopthalmia or Exophthalmos and can be caused by eye trauma or by fungal or bacterial infection / disease.

Trauma can be the result of a scrape, bump or a scratch. Fish can injure themselves on objects in the tank, get hurt during fights with other fish, and tank owners can accidentally damage fish's eyes when using an aquarium net. In the case of trauma, it is usually only one eye that is affected. An eye injury can look alarming but often doesn't impact on the overall health of the fish.

In the case of infections of some kind, the fish can be far more badly affected in terms of its general health and its ability and desire to feed. Both eyes may also be affected.

The third possible cause of eye problems, including eye infections, is a range of environmental factors such as:

- Poor water quality
- Contaminated items are introduced into the tank
- The water temperature is too high
- The levels of harmful compounds such as nitrates are above acceptable parameters
- The fish are stressed
- The fish are receiving poor or inadequate nutrition.

Symptoms

Popeye makes the eye look as though it is under pressure and bulging out of the head or about to pop out of the socket. Some of these conditions can also make the protruding eye look clouded or opaque. It can look a great deal worse or more serious than the case or condition is. What is significant is the underlying cause, as that must be addressed.

Treatment for trauma-induced Popeye

The affected fish poses no risk to the other fish in the main tank, as it is not infectious. Handling the fish will probably only worsen the injury. However, if the trauma is due to bullying by another fish, it would be wise to separate them. In addition, if the injury is severe, the fish must be placed in the quarantine tank for treatment.

Minor injuries will heal on their own over time, but treatment is required for more serious injuries. Aquarists recommend the use of a broad-spectrum antibiotic that is mixed into flake food. This will combat any infection that may start in the wound.

Using a liquid vitamin is also suggested and your vet or retailer will be able to advise you on the most appropriate products to use. Eventually the eye will return to normal size.

However, with more serious injuries or where treatment has not been effective, the fish may suffer very significant permanent effects. The fish may loose the sight in the affected eye. In this situation, the eye will look grey, opaque or even completely colourless.

With very severe eye injuries that go untreated, or where the treatment was not effective, the eye may disappear or burst. The shock and trauma of this can be fatal to the fish.

If both eyes are affected and the fish looses or partially looses its vision, it will be unable to feed properly and will not survive. Many tank owners prefer to use euthanasia rather than leave a blind fish to slowly and painfully starve to death.

Treatment for infection or disease induced Popeye

Popeye can also be a symptom, or one of the symptoms, of an underlying medical condition such as an internal fungal or bacterial infection such as Vibriosis or kidney disease. In these situations, both eyes are likely to be affected.

If the Popeye is treated rather than the underlying illness *and* the Popeye, then the eye condition naturally won't improve and the fish may die of the underlying medical issue or complications caused by it.

A fish with infection or disease-related Popeye must be removed from the general population and placed in a quarantine tank for treatment. Once in 'hospital', both medical issues can be dealt with.

If eye problems can be attributed to poor water quality, 5 to 10% of the tank water must be changed daily. The water must be tested regularly and steps taken to correct any problems. This routine must be continued until the eye conditions have cleared.

K) Vibriosis

Vibriosis is a bacterial disease that attacks the gastrointestinal tract / the digestive system. The bacterium that causes this illness is *Vibrio anguillarum* (*Vibrio anguillarium*). This is a serious and aggressive disease that progresses rapidly. Infection is the result of ingesting the bacteria in food.

Symptoms

Fish suffering from Vibriosis display a wide range of signs and symptoms. However, not all fish survive long enough to develop all of them.

Some signs are loss of appetite, lethargy, red or bloody streaks under the skin that become dark and swollen lesions that ooze pus, red spots on the body and cloudy eyes that may turn into Popeye. The tell-tale streaks and subsequent ulcers are the only symptom some fish display.

Treatment

Treatment must be given rapidly in an effort to save the fish that are infected and prevent further infections.

Fish with Vibriosis must be placed in a quarantine tank to avoid infecting their tank-mates. The sick fish and the water in the tank must be dosed with an antibiotic that will kill gram-negative bacteria (Erythromycin, for example). One must also use a broad-spectrum bactericide and Potassium Permanganate, as they will reduce the levels of free-floating bacteria in the water.

Increased salinity or specific gravity has no effect on the bacteria because it survives easily in saltwater. One must also do a 50% water change in the main tank as soon as possible. Find out from your vet what bactericide you can use in the main tank that won't affect corals and invertebrates adversely.

Preventing re-infection

Performing all the necessary routine maintenance on your tank will go a long way to helping avoid bacterial outbreaks in it. With Vibriosis changing the water and cleaning the substrate are the two most important tasks.

Using an effect detritus pack is also essential as these nasty bacteria eat uneaten food and waste material. They then thrive and are in turn eaten by the fish. For this reason, it is also very important not to over feed your fish so there is no uneaten food floating around.

Finally, keeping fish stress-free and using good quality food will keep your Betta fish's immune systems strong, which will make it easier for them to resist infection.

L) Ammonia Poisoning and Ammonia Burn

As the name implies, these are not illnesses or diseases but medical conditions caused by levels of ammonia in tank water that are far too high. These elevated levels are usually due to one or more of the following:

- Equipment malfunction or failure
- Loss of power
- The introduction of too many new fish and other creatures are introduced into the tank at one time and the filters can't cope
- Healthy bacteria in the tank have been lost as a result of medications in the water
- Sudden changes to water parameters.

Symptoms

With ammonia poisoning, the fish's gills become red and inflamed. Breathing is difficult and the fish gasps for air, often remaining at the surface of the water in an effort to ease the situation. Badly poisoned fish loose their appetites, become lethargic and may just lie on the bottom of the tank. Clamped fins may also be a symptom.

In the advanced stages of poisoning, red streaks and patches appear on the skin and fins. These begin to bleed, as do the gills. As tissues are further broken down, the fish begins to haemorrhage internally too and also suffers damage to the central nervous system. Fish suffering from ammonia poisoning will die if it is not treated very early.

With ammonia burn, there is redness and inflammation on the fins and tail.

Treatment

Treatment involves replacing 25 to 50 % of the water in the aquarium. In addition, the pH must be lowered so that the level is below 7.0. Fish that have been very badly poisoned can't be treated and will die. Euthanasia is a kinder option.

Prevention

The best methods to prevent ammonia poisoning and burn are to test the water regularly, avoid overcrowding in the tank, do regular water changes and make sure that all the essential equipment is working at all times. By doing these things, your fish won't become victims of this destructive chemical compound.

M) Dropsy

Dropsy is a symptom of a gram-negative bacterial infection of some kind and it is not a disease or illness in and of itself.

Bacterial infections are more common in fish with weak immune systems caused by stress from transportation, poor water quality including high ammonia or nitrate levels, inadequate nutrition or a marked drop in the temperature of the water.

Symptoms

The typical symptoms of dropsy are a very swollen or distended belly or abdomen and scales that stand out from the body. The scales can stick out almost at right angles to the body and can make the fish look a little like a pinecone. There are numerous symptoms caused by the underlying infections but these two are due to Dropsy itself.

Treatment

It is not easy to treat Dropsy, usually because the underlying infection causing it is so far advanced by this stage. As a result, some aquarists believe that the kindest thing to do is to euthanize affected fish. Treatment of Dropsy must in effect be one for the underlying bacterial condition. Affected fish must be placed in a quarantine tank and, once the bacteria concerned has been identified, dosed with a suitable antibiotic. The water's salinity levels are raised too (1 teaspoon per gallon is recommended).

A water change must be performed on the main tank to reduce the number of bacteria that may be present.

Prevention

In order to prevent Dropsy, one must prevent bacterial infections. The golden rule with that is to maintain a high level of water quality by performing all the necessary maintenance tasks.

Avoiding overfeeding and overcrowding is also important, as is a healthy and varied diet for all fish.

N) Hole in the Head (HITH) / Head and Lateral Line Erosion (HLLE)

The cause for this illness is not yet known or understood. The three most popular theories are that HITH or HLLE are caused by poor nutrition, long-term use of filters that use activated carbon and, finally, poor water quality. Other aquarists think that a lack of vitamins is a further contributing factor.

Symptoms

Fish suffering from HLLE develop indentations along the lateral line and on the head. It looks as though the tissue is breaking down. These indentations or pits worsen into holes or even open wounds, which can then become infected by bacteria. These fish loose their appetites and become very lethargic.

This condition progresses slowly and is not fatal. However, the effects on the fish's appetite and the secondary infections as a result of the HLLE are the killers, so the illness must still be taken seriously.

Treatment

HLLE requires a broad treatment approach because the causes are unknown. One therefore needs to cover all the possibilities:

- Do a water change and perform them regularly
- Ensure that their diet is optimal
- Add vitamins (Vitamins A, D, and E or the B range) or vitamin-enriched foods to their diet
- Iodine can also be a helpful supplement
- Use antibiotics *if* the fish is suffering from a secondary infection

- If you use carbon-based filtration either rinse it out very well or stop using it.

O) Nitrite / Nitrate Poisoning

Nitrate or Nitrite poisoning is also called Brown Blood Disease. As the name indicates, this is not a disease but a serious and potentially fatal medical condition brought about by fish being affected / poisoned by elevated levels of nitrates in the water.

One of the lead causes of Nitrate / Nitrite poisoning is a bio-load that is far heavier than the filtration and other tank systems can cope with or following a failure of the filtration system or a prolonged power loss.

Symptoms

There is a range of symptoms that will assist a tank owner to diagnose this form of poisoning in fish, even if testing the nitrate levels in the tank is not enough to indicate this.

The milder symptoms include lethargy and very limited movement, with affected fish tending to stay just below the water surface. Poisoned fish gasp for air and may remain near the surface or water outlets. The gills move very rapidly and loose their normal pink or red colour and turn brown.

The name Brown Blood Disease stems from the increase in levels of methemoglobin in the blood, which literally turns it brown. The even more serious aspect of this rise in methemoglobin is that the blood becomes unable to transport oxygen. Fish, in effect, suffocate to death. It also results in damage to, and loss of, blood cells and organ damage too.

Treatment

The single most important intervention is an immediate water change. Nitrate levels must be tested and watched very closely. Further partial water changes must be done as necessary. In fact, more water changes are necessary the larger the population of the tank.

One also needs to increase the rate of aeration and add chlorine salt (ideally) or aquarium salt to the water. If the affected fish are not eating well or at all you must reduce the amount of food you put in the tank. Uneaten food will add to the problems.

This regimen must be continued until you get nitrate readings of zero.

Prevention

Performing the necessary routine maintenance, not over feeding or overstocking and testing nitrate levels regularly are the very best ways to prevent a lethal build-up of this toxic compound in the tank water.

In the case of a new tank, the stock should be introduced slowly so that the systems can adjust and accommodate them and toxic compounds such as nitrates don't begin to build up. Levels should be tested regularly.

A red flag for nitrate level problems is an increase in ammonia levels. If your tests pick up raised ammonia, there is every chance that, unless you take immediate corrective steps, a nitrate increase will follow very soon.

P) Oxygen Starvation

While poisoning results from an intake of a harmful substance, this condition is the result of fish not getting enough oxygen due to inadequate water aeration or gas exchange at the surface of the water.

Symptoms

As would be expected with a lack of oxygen, the main symptom is that affected fish will gasp for air, sometimes with their mouths above the surface of the water. Fish often appear to be gulping and the gills move very quickly.

Treatment

The most obvious 'fix' is to increase the levels of aeration, and therefore oxygen, in the tank by increasing airflow and the speed of water circulation through the filters.

Aquarists also suggest that one check the water temperature. If the temperature goes up the oxygen requirements go up too. If you find that the water is too warm, it's vital to bring it down to normal levels as quickly as possible. Using the cooling or chilling methods described in an earlier chapter will prove useful and will bring relief to the fish, as oxygen becomes available in the water once more.

Q) External Bubble Disease

This condition is not infectious and is due entirely to one of two environmental factors: too much oxygen or too much water pressure.

The symptoms are dramatic and alarming but often the condition resolves itself. If it doesn't, it can be treated and managed fairly easily.

Symptoms

As the name suggests, the main symptom are gas-filled bubbles that are clearly visible and form on the outside of the fish's body or on the eyes or fins. In extreme cases, the bubbles are so large that the fish floats, unable to swim.

Although fish that are affected by Bubble Disease can suffer permanent damage to skin, eyes (even loss of an eye or blindness) or fins, it is not often a fatal condition. The exception is when bubbles also form internally, as they can cause organs to rupture or fail. This is rare, fortunately. The other complicating factor is bacterial infections in tissue after the bubbles have popped.

Treatment

The treatment that is administered is dependent on which of the two causes are responsible for the formation of these bubbles. In either case, however, the bubbles must *not* be popped as this leaves the fish vulnerable to infection as it causes an opening into the skin, fin or eye, and it causes pain!

If the cause is oxygen super-saturation, the water temperature in the tank probably needs to be raised. Although it won't happen immediately, the warming water will release the extra oxygen into the air above the water surface. One needs to monitor the temperature very carefully so that the water does not become too warm, as this will stress the fish and also drop oxygen levels too low, which will then lead to oxygen starvation and suffocation.

If, on the other hand, the condition is due to pressure, one needs to depressurise the fish. This is usually only found in wild-caught fish that were living at depth and were brought to the surface too fast. The bubbles of oxygen in their bodies are forced to the surface, where they form bubbles.

In the unlikely event of a Betta fish with pressure-induced Bubble Disease, you need to place it as deep in the aquarium as you can and keep in at that depth until the symptoms begin to ease.

Prevention

The best way to guard against Bubble Disease in Betta fish is to buy captive-bred specimens and to ensure that water temperatures and oxygen / aeration levels are as they should be at all times.

R) Swim Bladder Disorder

This occurs quite often in *Betta splendens.* The good news is that it is not contagious. The cause is overfeeding or feeding young fish / fry in particular the incorrect foods. Stress can also cause this disorder in older fish.

Symptoms

The swim bladder is located between the tail and the belly, next to the spine and is involved in swimming and flotation. The primary symptom is that fish that are affected have great difficulty swimming.

If the swim bladder is swollen then the fish will float helplessly on one side, often on the bottom of the tank. A swim bladder that is too short causes the fish to be unable to swim horizontally.

Treatment

Bettas often recover spontaneously but reducing food intake can help a great deal because the correlation between overfeeding and swim bladder disorder is so strong. Brine shrimp are thought to be the greatest culprit, so one could consider removing them from the menu all together or using them far less often.

Euthanasia of these fish is not an option because of the high rates of spontaneous recovery. It's also not necessary to place these fish in quarantine, as they are not contagious at any stage. The other good news is that this condition is not painful.

S) Possible Depression

Yes, fish get depressed too. The signs are that a fish may appear under the weather but has no distinct set of symptoms. If one can rule out bacterial infection or internal parasites, chances are the Betta is unhappy.

Males exhibit this problem after being separated from its fry. Young fish can be depressed after being separated from its dozens of siblings. The adjustment is evidently difficult.

Symptoms

Fish usually stop eating and they become far less active. They may also have clamped fins. Males stop building bubble nests, too. If they continue to refuse to eat, death will inevitably follow.

Treatment

An initial action to adopt with any Betta or other fish that seems ill is to carry out a water change, as this can often help. One can also add a few drops of broad-spectrum medication in case the cause is a mild bacterial infection.

If it is a very young Betta you could reintroduce it to other fish the same size and age so it has company. An adult male that has just finished the spawning and hatching process can benefit from being floated in a suitable container in a tank with another Betta, preferably a female.

T) Inflamed Gills

The causes of this condition are bacterial infection, nitrate poisoning or some sort of defect – usually congenital or a birth defect – within the gill itself.

Symptoms

The primary symptom is that the affected gill does not close properly. This is easier to see if you watch the sick fish from above rather than from the side. The gills often look very red or inflamed and may even be swollen.

The final stage of this very serious condition is that the fish will battle to breathe. It can be seen to be gasping for air. As it is a labyrinth fish it can get some oxygen through its mouth at the water surface but not enough.

These fish will eventually die and it is an unpleasant, slow death. Some hobbyists choose to euthanize the affected fish.

Treatment

As with most illnesses and health problems, the first step must be to do a water change. An antibiotic solution must be added to the treatment water.

If the cause is nitrate poisoning, the fish will get more relief from methylene blue and not antibiotics.

3) A fish First Aid Kit

While one can't prepare for every eventuality, it is a good idea to keep a first aid kit on hand so you can treat your Betta fish and other creatures immediately if the need arises. Some illnesses are so aggressive that waiting for your vet or a shop to open the next day or Monday morning is simply not an option!

One should also invest in a basic *Betta splendens* first aid kit, as getting the right medications when they are needed is often difficult or impossible as they are not all sold by retailers or, sometimes, even by vets. A kit could contain:

- Aquarium Salt
- PIMAfix
- Splendid Betta BettaFix Remedy or MELAfix
- Betta Revive or equivalent
- QuICK Cure or equivalent
- Jungle's Parasite Clear Tank Buddies or equivalent
- Jungle's Fungus Clear Tank Buddies or equivalent
- An anti-stress solution
- Maracyn and Maracyn 2 or equivalent
- Parasite Clear or equivalent
- Fungus Clear or equivalent.

It's important to check the contents of the kit regularly to make sure that none of the medications or solutions are past their expiry dates. If they are, they must be replaced immediately. In addition, as you finish something you need to purchase more. You don't want to discover you have run out of a life-saving item at the time you really need it!

A quarantine tank is of course a very big part of a tank owner's ability to prevent health problems and deal effectively with them when, not if, they do occur.

4) Pet insurance

If you use a quarantine tank, follow good maintenance routines and schedules to ensure high quality water, and use high quality foods to strengthen immunity, your Betta fish and other tank inhabitants should stay pretty healthy. However, fish are prone to illness and even the healthiest creature can be injured.

Enter pet insurance. It used to be that pet insurance only catered for dogs and cats. In a very recent development, there are now some insurers that will cover fish. One would have to establish which companies offer this option.

With standard insurance there is a choice of a plan that covers expenses in the event of an accident only. Others will pay costs for both accident and illness. Your vet should be able to supply you with a brochure, pamphlet or information. You will have to weigh the cost of insurance against the possibility of being out of pocket at a later date.

Like most insurance, these policies will have a deductible or excess that you will have to pay, but they can help greatly if your tank creatures ever require vet care in the form of tests and / or medications. The premium and affordability will also vary depending on the type of cover chosen.

Chapter 12: Breeding Betta fish

Betta splendens are bred commercially and have been for a very long time indeed. The captive breeding programmes of these popular fish have been very successful and, as seen in an earlier chapter, have resulted in an array of beautiful colours and fin and tail shapes and sizes. Some breeders say that if you want to breed your Bettas, you need an established pair or a mated pair rather than buying a single female and a male. However, most aquarists don't believe that this is necessary with this species.

Once you have your breeding pair, there are things you can do to encourage them to spawn – such as keeping the quality of the water high – and, later, ways to help as many of the hatchlings to survive as possible.

1) Sexual maturity

Once you have a mating pair of *Betta splendens* they will need to be in a stable tank environment that offers them good quality water. These fish reach sexual maturity quite early: when they are 4 to 5 months old.

2) Spawning

Bettas start to look and act differently around spawning time. Females become darker in colour and develop stripes on their bodies and both males and females engage in courtship movements.

Males flare their gills, spread their fins and twist their bodies to show their tails and fins to best effect. An interested female will move her body back and forth in response to the male's courtship 'dance'.

When it is time to spawn, the male builds a nest made of bubbles and often uses a plant or rock surface as the base for the nest. All the nests are built at the surface of the water and they vary in both size and density. Interestingly, healthy mature males will build bubble nests regularly throughout adulthood even if there is no female.

Once the bubble nest is ready and the female is receptive, spawning begins. The male wraps his body around the female and gives her what is called the "nuptial embrace". With each 'hug' the female releases between 12 and 40 eggs into the water. The male continues to embrace the female until she no longer produces eggs. The female will produce 400 to 600 eggs each spawning. The male releases milt, or sperm, into the water after each embrace and the eggs are fertilized externally.

The male, sometimes with the help of the female, collects the eggs in his mouth and deposits them into the bubble nests he had prepared. More usually, the male collects the eggs and chases off the female when spawning is over because she may eat the eggs.

3) Caring for the eggs

The male remains with and cares for the eggs with the female having no further involvement at all. He ensures that the eggs remain safely in the bubble nest by keeping it strong and doing any necessary repairs so that the eggs don't fall out of the bottom of the nest.

Once the larvae and fry have all left the nest, the male should be removed from the tank as he may eat the babies. Be careful not to accidentally catch any fry in the net when you take the male out or damage the delicate bubble nest.

The other thing you need to check for is any larvae or fry that may be in the male's mouth if you caught him as he was transporting babies back to the next. To check for this place him in a jar or keep him in the net at the water's surface so that he has a chance to spit his offspring out. Don't place him back in the main tank with the female *Betta splendens* and / or other fish until you have checked this or the young that he releases will certainly be eaten.

Some aquarists treat the male with a product such as Bettamax for a few days after removing him from the hatching tank. As unlikely as it may sound, many males are prone to depression and illness when separated from their fry.

4) The hatching tank

It is best not to allow the eggs to hatch in the main tank, where they will most likely be eaten by other fish. Ideally, you need to remove the eggs about two days before they hatch and place them in a dedicated tank.

A hatching or rearing tank only needs to be a small (10 gallons or 45.5 UK litres or 37 US litres), although you can use a larger one if you choose to do so. These tanks, like quarantine tanks, can be sparse in terms of equipment. All that is necessary is a heater or heating mat, a small air-stone and a pump. There is no need for substrate or any tank décor.

The lighting used should not be too bright. It is essential that you don't install a filter or filtration system of any kind in a hatching tank. The fry are very small and delicate and filters will injure or even kill them.

What is essential is that the pH level and temperature of the water are as close to those in the main tank as possible. Some aquarists recommend that one exchanges half of the fresh water from the hatching tank with that of the main aquarium so that the water conditions are as close as possible.

Once the hatching tank is ready it is time to transfer the eggs into it from the main tank. The ideal scenario is removing the eggs along with the rock or plant they are on. Because the eggs must not on any account come into contact with air, you need to place the rock into a suitable transfer container under the water.

5) Hatching

After an incubation period of 24 to 36 hours (depending on water temperature) the eggs hatch and the Betta larvae that emerge remain in the bubble nest until they have absorbed all the nutrition from the yolk sac in the egg. This takes 2 or 3 days, during which time they hang upside down from the nest.

The larvae tend to wriggle and often fall out of the nest. The male will retrieve them and return them to the safety of the nest. If the male does not collect them all – and it can be impossible for him – there is no need for concern. Even if the male does not fetch them, they can safely lie on the bottom until they can swim up to the nest themselves or the reach the next stage of their development and simply swim off.

At this point the larvae have grown into free-swimming fry or baby fish and they leave the nest. It will take a further 3 to 6 weeks before these hatchlings develop their labyrinth organs and they only breathe with their gills.

Even experienced aquarists are not able to successfully raise all the fry. One may need to siphon out all the dead, deformed and weak fry. The behaviour of dying fry or baby fish is hard to miss. They struggle to swim and may just spin in currents in the tank. Others will simply sink to the bottom of the tank, try to swim and then sink again. Fry or hatchlings behaving in this manner are unlikely to survive for more than a day. Either a siphon pipe or a pipette can be used to remove the dead or dying young.

Healthy, just hatched fry are often hungry. One way to boost the survival rate is to place suitable food in the hatching tank so the baby fish can begin to feed.

While the larvae and fry are still in, and later suspended under, the nest they are feeding from their egg sac and don't need any other food. However, once they are horizontal and free swimming they need to be fed, and quickly.

Betta splendens fry, like most, far prefer live, moving food. The movement also serves to stimulate the development of necessary mouth and swallowing movement and reflexes in the young. But because the fish are so small, the food must also be small!

Betta breeders must prepare these cultures before the eggs are laid, never mind before the free-swimming fry are ready for food. There are several options: infusoria, Paramecium Aurelia, micro worms, baby brine shrimp and Vinegar eels.

6) Cultures for feeding fry

Infusoria

Infusoria are tiny microorganisms that are ideal for very small fry. Creating a culture of millions of these organisms is not hard.

- Siphon water from the bottom of the main or an established tank that, preferably, contains plants
- Put this water in large glass jars. Properly cleaned and rinsed pickle or other food jars work well
- Place a few dead aquatic plant leaves in the water or even an animal food pellet that is made of plant material only
- Leave the jars in bright light for a few weeks
- Remove the literally millions of Infusoria out of the jars as they are needed to feed the fry using a dropper or pipette. Some hobbyists mix this water with crushed hard boiled egg yolk or egg powder

- Only a few drops of this highly nutritious liquid is needed to feed medium sized fry
- This is an excellent food source for the first week of the free-swimming fry's lives.

Paramecium aurelia

This is considered more as a supplementary rather than a main food for fry. Paramecium is a single-celled protozoan that is good for slightly larger fry.

The items one needs to create a culture are a starter culture (obtainable from good retailers), Liquifry or an equivalent product for egg-layers and a small glass container. As with Infusoria, the solution should be left in the bright light but only for a few days. A small cup of the culture will keep fry happy for some days.

However, there are aquarists that believe very strongly that this solution is just a way to introduce millions of bacteria into a tank and is not necessary for the feeding of fry at all.

Vinegar Eel or Turbatrix aceti

The name is misleading, as these are not eels at all but tiny nematodes or minute roundworms. Nematodes are considered to be an excellent first food for older fry.

Further advantages are that these 'eels' swim in the water and are not bottom-dwellers and this makes it easy for the growing baby Bettas to find and catch them. In addition, these organisms last a few days in tank water, so there is no need for more than one feeding of these nematodes every 3 or 4 days.

Culturing these eels is also not hard. Use a clean jar or a jug into which you have placed half an apple. Add apple cider vinegar (1/3) and cool water (1/3) and then the contents of a packet of culture starter. The container should be covered and then left for 4 to 5 weeks.

The nematodes should be visible to the naked eye and look like fine, thread-like worms. They can be harvested from the liquid using a piece of muslin or even a filter coffee paper to strain them out. Rinse the cloth or paper in clean water to get the nematodes off and then feed them to the fry using a dropper.

Micro worms

These are slightly larger than Vinegar Eels and are an excellent source of food for older fry. One can buy micro worm cultures, which are placed and kept in suitable mediums. Easy ones for most *Betta splendens* owners are damp bread, cornmeal, oatmeal or damp and fine ground porridge or cereal products.

The medium should be damp or even wet before you add the culture and a small pinch of baker's yeast. Place it in a container with a secure lid.

In just a few days you will have thousands of worms crawling around. The lid will make sure the fish food doesn't escape! These worms can be removed with cotton wool, a finger or a damp and soft cloth.

Brine Shrimp or Artemia nauplii

One can buy Brine Shrimp hatcheries, most of which consist of a stand and a pipe so that a small aerator can be attached. The final item one needs to use is a two litre (½ gallon) plastic bottle or other suitable container. Retailers supply packets of Brine Shrimp eggs and salt for inclusion in the water.

The container should be filled to a few inches below the rim. The supplied salt should be mixed into prepared water. Once the aerator hose has been placed into the container, one can simply pour the Brine Shrimp eggs into the water. The eggs will hatch in 24 to 48 hours.

The shells left behind after Brine Shrimp have hatched are brown and they float, often to the surface of the water in the hatchery. The hatched shrimps, on the other hand, stay at the bottom. This makes it much easier to remove the shells, which can't and shouldn't be used as food. The eggs can be skimmed off using a suitable net or a pipette.

The Brine Shrimp that you have grown should only be kept for 3 or 4 days after they have hatched. This means that you need to place eggs in the hatchery on a staggered basis so that there are always newly hatched shrimp for your Betta fry to eat.

7) Feeding older Betta fry

Fry that have reached about 2 weeks of age are ready for changes or additions to their diets and some frozen foods such as daphnia (tiny crustaceans) can be introduced.

When the babies are a month old, they can be introduced to freeze-dried foods in addition to frozen and live ones. Keep in mind, however, that frozen foods must be chopped up and defrosted before being given to the fry.

The menu at this point could include brine shrimp, daphnia and bloodworms. One can also introduce small dried food granules. Keep the golden rule in mind and don't overfeed the fry.

8) Growing hatchlings

You now have a hatching tank containing young *Betta splendens* and you are culturing food and keeping the young fish well fed. What else do you need to do to keep the growing fry healthy and strong?

As with adult fish and the main tank, water changes are vital when it comes to caring for hatchlings and fry. Many breeders suggest that one remove and replace 50% of the water in the hatching tank twice a week. If there is a smaller number, for instance 50 babies in 10 gallons, in a tank then once a week should be adequate.

As the fry grow, the frequency will have to increase. If there is no filter in the tank the changes will be more frequent. One has to use one's best judgement so that water stays clean and of a good quality at all times.

You must also ensure that the substrate stays clean because young fry spend a lot of their time at the bottom. If there is uneaten food and other waste matter around them they are likely to contract a bacterial infection, which could spread to the rest of the fry.

Once Betta fry begin to move to the surface to begin to breathe there too as their labyrinth organs develop, you also need to make sure the water's surface is clean and clear.

At about the age of 4 months the young fish begin to exhibit their adult colours and there will be a greater range of sizes as some fry grow faster than others. Cannibalizing of the small fry by the bigger ones is not unheard of and can upset some hobbyists. Not much can be done to prevent it, however, other than separating them by placing smaller fish in one container and the larger ones in another.

As the young Bettas grow, and this is rapid in this point of their development, you may need to place them in a larger or multiple tanks to avoid overcrowding and fights.

At 6 to 8 weeks the colours and fins will have developed to the point that one can tell which fish are male and which are female.

Some breeders separate young males and females but others keep them together until they are a little older. One really needs to decide based on how the maturing fish interact with each other.

9) Re-homing baby Betta fish

Raising *Betta splendens* fry is a lot of work but managing to do so successfully is really exciting and very rewarding. However, what if you can't or don't want to keep them all?

You really only have two options. You can sell them privately but this presents real problems unless you know how to safely ship fish. The second option is to approach a dealer. Retailers are often interested in acquiring healthy Betta fish when they are about 0.5 inches or 1.25 centimetres.

On the down side you are unlikely to be paid much for them. An alternative that some breeders opt for is to be given credit or goods by the supplier in exchange for fry.

Chapter 13: Prices, costs & where to buy Betta fish

1) Costs

The cost of purchasing a Betta:

These amazing fish are not as costly as one would expect. A *Betta splendens* will set you back between £3 / $4.75 and £9.70 / $15. On top of that you will need to pay for all the equipment you will need before you can even take your new pet home.

Set-up costs:

You need certain basic equipment for your Betta fish. These once-off costs include:

- Tank or aquarium: depending on size and design the prices range from $55 / £37 to $2000 / £1349. Some of these prices include a hood or cover and an under-substrate filter. The very expensive tanks may include housing such as a cabinet and a number of pieces of equipment.
- Substrate: $9 – 39 / £6 – 26
- Rocks: $22 – 30 / £15 – 20
- Plants: $5 – 80 / £3.20 – 52
- Algae sheets or attack pack: $3 – 16 / £2 – 11
- Filter: $ 5.50 – 25 / £4 – 17
- Thermometer: $2.75 – 18 / £1.85 – 12
- Powerhead: $22 – 70 / £15 – 47
- Wave makers and oscillators: $176 – 296 / £119 – 200
- Heater: $29 – 38.50 / £ 19 – 26
- Protein skimmer: $89 – 281 / £60 – 190
- Full spectrum light: $6 – 296 / £4 – 200
- Water conditioner: $2 – 13 / £1.35 – 9
- Hydrometer: $9 – 17 / £6 – 11.25
- Refractometer: $12 / £8
- Detritus attack pack: $39 – 160 / £26.30 – 108

- Water test kit: $14.50 – 40 / £10 – 27
- Water filter: $13 – 150 / £8.50 – 101
- Carbon filtration system: $89 – 218 / £60 – 147.50
- Reverse Osmosis (RO) or Deionization (DI) filtration unit: $123 – 388 / £83 – 262
- UV Steriliser: $16 – 297 / £11 – 200

These are just for a single tank or aquarium. Additional tanks and a few of the most basic items will be necessary for a hatching, growing-on and quarantine tank.

You may be able to buy items, including second-hand or pre-owned ones, more cheaply online but then you need to think about how clean these items might be. The last thing you want is to acquire a tank that is infected with bacteria, a virus or a parasite that will infect all your stock.

Ongoing, regular costs:

These expenses include all the items you need for regular, routine maintenance and hygiene and for the overall health and well being of your Betta fish and other tank inhabitants.

- Aquarium salt mix: $22 – 74 / £15 – 50
- Aquarium nets: $4 – 6 / £3 – 4
- Aquarium brushes: $11 / £7.50
- Flake food: $5 – 11 / £3.30 – 7.25
- Brine Shrimp eggs: $12 – 16 / £8 – 10.80

These regular costs obviously don't include any emergencies or unforeseen 'extras' that you may encounter such as vet bills for tests, for example. They also don't include the items that go into the first aid kit, which will depend on how many items you purchase and which brand you select.

2) Where you can buy a Betta splendens

Buying equipment from more general or non-specialist retailers is usually fine. However, one needs to be careful about where one buys the fish themselves.

One doesn't want to obtain specimens that are sold as captive-bred but are in actual fact wild caught. In addition, less specialised retailers may, deliberately or inadvertently, sell fish that are close to the end of their life span or sick.

You could ask a vet who includes fish in his or her practise for recommendations about local breeders. Do research on the Internet. Joining Betta fish groups, clubs and forums online is a wonderful way to find information.

There are shops that one can visit and a large number of reputable on-line specialist shops where one can buy fish that will be shipped safely.

Chapter 14: Conclusion

1) Do's… in no particular order

- ✓ Learn about *Betta splendens* and aquarium care
- ✓ Find out what fish and other species are compatible and can share a tank
- ✓ Make sure you get a tank that is large enough
- ✓ Buy captive-bred fish rather than wild-caught fish
- ✓ Observe fish carefully to look for signs of ill-health before buying a fish
- ✓ Take the time to set up the aquarium or tank properly
- ✓ Include an algae attack pack
- ✓ Make use of a detritus attack pack
- ✓ Invest in good quality tank equipment
- ✓ Buy and equip a smaller tank that will be used as a quarantine or hospital tank
- ✓ Ensure that the water quality of always good
- ✓ Draw up a maintenance schedule
- ✓ Perform regular maintenance
- ✓ Check and meet all the necessary water and tank parameters (salinity, pH, temperature, calcium, phosphates, etc.)
- ✓ Take the time to acclimate all creatures using either the float or the drip method before placing them in a tank
- ✓ Be prepared for a loss of power

- ✓ Feed your fish a balanced, healthy diet
- ✓ Keep a First Aid Kit
- ✓ Quarantine new-comers
- ✓ Only feed larvae and fry the food they are ready for and need at each stage of growth.

2) Don'ts… in no particular order

- Use tap water
- Use common table salt
- Fail to test water parameters regularly
- Neglect routine maintenance tasks including performing water replacements
- Introduce unwashed / rinsed rocks and other décor into the aquarium
- Rush the vital acclimation process
- Feed Bettas fatty foods
- Overfeed fish
- Place too many fish in a tank so you have over crowding which causes stress
- Ignore signs of ill-health
- Neglect to make contingency plans for in the event of a power failure
- Leave fish unattended in the treatment bath or the dip
- Leave the female in with the eggs or the male with the larvae.

3) A reminder of the Big Mistakes that cost!

One needs to take being a *Betta splendens* owner seriously. This commitment must begin before you even bring your new pet home. These creatures are entirely dependent on the tank owner and he or she can't decide to take a few days off or go away without making provision for the care of the aquarium.

An aquarium is a "closed system" and without due care the creatures in it will not survive. An aquarist or hobbyist must take the time and trouble to become informed by learning about the species and about caring for tanks.

The main reason that fish die in tanks – as a rule – is because owners are either ignorant or don't care for the inhabitants properly. The primary causes of aquarium fish death are:

Improper or no acclimation

It's not enough to acclimate new fish to water temperature alone because this is just one of the important environmental factors. Fish also need to be acclimated to the pH. The shock of a sudden change in pH can kill fish that are particularly sensitive to this particular parameter.

Incorrect diet or insufficient food

If fish, like any other living creature, don't receive enough food they will become malnourished and weak. Their immune systems are then affected and fish are far less likely to be able to fend off or fight an infection or infestation. If there is no food provided, fish will starve to death rapidly, especially very young fish.

In addition to not being given enough food, being fed the wrong diet is also a big problem. Either the fish simply won't eat a food item that they are unfamiliar with or can't cope with or they will eat it and be adversely affected by it.

Overfeeding

As much as too little food is harmful so is too much food.

Firstly, uneaten food that remains in the tank will seriously compromise water quality. As has been discussed, poor water quality is responsible for a host of problems and illnesses including very serious ones.

Some individual fish will gorge themselves and this can be fatal.

Contamination of the aquarium and stock

Not using a quarantine tank can be disastrous. Fish may appear healthy and a retailer may supply specimens in good faith but they may be carrying parasites including ones that cause very serious illness such as Cryptocaryon and Oodinium. Not only will the infected fish require treatment, which may or may not be successful, but also all the fish in the tank might become infected.

Using a quarantine tank will usually save your fish from illness and suffering and you from a great deal of work, expense and distress.

Poor water quality

Fish must have a stable environment that stays within certain set parameters. These are non-negotiable and include the correct levels or total absence of certain compounds, pH and salinity levels, oxygenation levels and temperature. Not testing these parameters regularly will prove very costly to you and your fish and any other creatures in the tank.

If water is not of high quality the fish become stressed and this weakens their immune systems and their bodies generally. This leaves them vulnerable to attack by bacteria, viruses and parasites.

Good water quality is not difficult to maintain if one prepares water properly, does not overfeed, and one carries out all of the necessary maintenance tasks properly and as often as necessary. This includes the very important partial water changes, which offer so many benefits. This maintenance would also include ensuring that vital equipment such as filters and skimmers are working, as they should.

Species incompatibility

Not all fish species get on well together and this is especially true of the bettas as they are territorial and aggressive fish.

Part of the all-important homework that must be done before setting up an aquarium is to examine compatibility so that the residents of your aquarium get on and don't attack each other or become stressed.

4) Health specific Do's and Don'ts

Do's:

- ✓ Quarantine all new fish or other creatures before introducing them into a tank or aquarium
- ✓ Always monitor the health of all your fish regularly
- ✓ Keep the water clean
- ✓ Ensure the tank is large enough
- ✓ Use aquarium salt
- ✓ Remove sick or dead fish immediately
- ✓ Trim plants regularly
- ✓ Isolate and treat sick fish without delay
- ✓ Wash your hands and disinfect any item that has come into contact with a sick or dead fish to prevent contamination
- ✓ Have a *Betta splendens* first aid kit available

Don'ts:

- Don't subject fish to sudden changes in water conditions
- Don't overfeed your fish or fry
- Don't make a tank or aquarium too crowded
- Don't leave uneaten food and other waste in the tank

5) And in closing…

This guide's primary purpose is to make sure that you have the information that you need to decide, first and foremost, if this is really the right pet for you, for your spouse, or for your child.

If the answer is a confident and honest "Yes", this pet owner's guide will also give you the details that will help you to keep your Betta fish healthy and happy.

All animals in captivity should at least live to their usual or expected life span. In fact, given they are safe from their natural predators and receive a good diet and vet care they should exceed the average life span for their species.

If you are one of those individuals who commits to owning and caring for one of these amazing fish you will be rewarded by having a pet that is fascinating, beautiful, and rewarding! Enjoy your Betta fish and teach others about them.

Published by IMB Publishing 2015

19512925R00072

Printed in Great Britain
by Amazon